Adopting
the
Racing
Greyhound

Also by Cynthia A. Branigan

The Reign of the Greyhound: A Popular History of the Oldest Family of Dogs

second edition

Adopting
the
Racing
Greyhound

CYNTHIA A. BRANIGAN

HOWELL BOOK HOUSE

New York

The purpose of this book is to provide information for those adopting and caring for an ex-racing Greyhound. The Publisher and/or the Author shall not be responsible for any injuries or damage incurred by following the information given in this book.

Copyright © 1992, 1998 by Cynthia A. Branigan

Photograph on dedication page by Ann G. Krisher

Howell Book House

Published by Wiley Publishing, Inc., New York, NY

For general information on our other products and services, please contact our Customer Care Department within the U.S. at 800-762-2974, outside the U.S. at 317-572-3993 or fax 317-572-4002.

Wiley also publishes its books in a variety of electronic formats. Some content that appears in print may not be available in electronic books.

Library of Congress Cataloging-in-Publication data

Branigan, Cynthia A.
Adopting the racing greyhound/Cynthia A. Branigan. –2nd ed.
p.cm.
Includes bibliographical references and index
ISBN 0-87605-193-x
1. Racing greyhound.   2. Dog adoption.   I. Title.
SF429,G8B73   1998   97-53092
636.753'4–de21   CIP

Manufactured in the United States of America
10 9 8 7 6 5

Book Design: Scott Meola
Cover Design: Kevin Hanek

*This book is dedicated, with love and gratitude, to
KING (Low Key Two)
Without whose gentle spirit and inspiration
This book could not have been written.
The work continues in his name . . .*

(Photo: Ann G. Krisher)

Contents

Foreword

It isn't every author of a foreword to a book who will tell you to beware. But I am doing so. I am not saying, mind you, to beware of the dog because this book is about one of the most endearing breeds of dog in the world. Nor am I saying to beware this book—which is one of the most thorough manuals of adoption that has ever been my pleasure to read. What I am doing, however, is saying to beware of the author.

I first met Cynthia Branigan nearly twenty years ago when she was a newspaper reporter in Philadelphia. Since that time I have known her as a friend and long-time fellow worker at The Fund for Animals. I am telling you this because The Fund for Animals specialized in the rescue of all kinds of animals—wild burros from the Grand Canyon, wild goats from San Clemente Island, wild horses, wild pigs and even the last Atlantic City Steel Pier Diving Horses. I learned early on that Cynthia, who loved all animals, was also a marvelous adopter of all animals. Indeed whatever animal we rescued, Cynthia could and would find the right person to adopt it.

I remember well the day Cynthia told me she had fallen in love with a dog. I knew she had been working with Greyhound rescue and had in fact set up her own society for that task—so I asked her if the object of her affection was a Greyhound. She said it was. His name, she said, was King. With that she poured out paean of praise and superlatives about not only King in particular and the entire Greyhound breed in general but also why everyone, man, woman and child, should have one.

I am, of course, kidding to ask you to beware this woman. Cynthia is much too much of a professional to want anyone to adopt an animal who is likely to be incompatible with that animal. Instead, as her book makes amply clear, she is just as interested in whether you are right for the dog you think you want to adopt as in whether that dog is right for you.

This book goes into virtually every conceivable situation that a person adopting a Greyhound is likely to encounter. But with its completeness the book is also extraordinarily readable, including both the proud history of this oldest of all purebred dog families as well as fascinating individual stories from people across the country who have decided for humanitarian reasons, or for the simple desire for companionship, to adopt.

Don't think I'm going to let the beware idea go completely, though. It is true Cynthia leans over backward to point out the adjustments and even difficulties you may have. But somehow in between the lines of these cautions you can read clear as crystal Cynthia's deep and abiding love for these creatures. "Don't worry," she is saying, "go ahead. You will not regret it."

CLEVELAND AMORY

$\mathcal{P}$reface to the $\mathcal{S}$econd Edition

When *Adopting the Racing Greyhound* was first published in the fall of 1992, my publisher, Sean Frawley, took a chance that the book would be of enough interest to the dog-loving public that it would at least pay for the cost of the first printing. Happily, it did and as of this writing there have been twelve printings of the first edition and it has sold over 70,000 copies. While it would be fun to take all of the credit for the book's remarkable success, I cannot. The real credit goes to the Greyhounds themselves.

A scant ten years ago, ownership of an ex-racing Greyhound was a rarity. Those of us who were lucky enough to have one were often stopped and asked either "What kind of dog is that?" or "Is that a Whippet?" Those days are long gone and now it is quite common for the owner of a Greyhound to be congratulated on saving a dog and, just as often, to be asked where one can be adopted. This is a breed that sells itself with its gentle and affectionate nature.

Looking back over the six years that have passed since the first edition of *Adopting the Racing Greyhound* appeared, I realize that there have been some significant changes for these dogs. For one thing, fewer Greyhounds are destroyed than ever before. Approximately 16,000 found homes in 1997 through the efforts of adoption groups across the country. And while some 20,000 were destroyed, that figure is greatly decreased from six years ago when it hovered around the 40,000 mark. The racing industry has made a concerted effort to decrease the number of breedings (and hence reduce the number of dogs needing homes to begin with) and they have also supported many adoption efforts. For this they are to be commended. While all of us involved in placing these dogs look forward to the day when no Greyhounds are destroyed, I believe we must acknowledge that progress is being made.

Another big change is the number of adoption groups that have sprouted up in the last six years. In the first edition of this book I listed all known agencies in the United States and Canada that placed retired racers: 60 entries. Today there are over 225 agencies, including ones in England, Ireland and Australia, which means more dogs can be placed than ever before. Let's hope this leads to further cooperation between groups and the realization of our common goal—to find responsible, loving homes for these dogs.

On the medical front there have been some advances made that make life easier for both people and dogs. There was once a time when ticks and their fellow pests, fleas, presented a major headache to all dog owners. Not so anymore. There are now new products on the market that can just about eliminate both of these. Of special interest to Greyhound owners, though, is the fact that most of these new products are safe for our breed.

Over time it has been discovered that many Greyhounds have been exposed to disease-carrying ticks. While this is not good news, it is good that we are now aware of it. Many groups are now either tick testing in advance or offering the service at a nominal fee. These tick-borne diseases are treatable if caught early, so the responsible owner will want to read up on this and take the appropriate measures.

Through my own adoption group I have, so far, been involved directly with the adoption of over 2,500 Greyhounds. All of these experiences have led me to believe that there is a need for even more information about the many ways to ease the transition from racing dog to family pet. This is especially true for adopters with children. This subject is expanded in this second edition and I am confident it will help new adopters, adoption groups, and most importantly, the Greyhounds.

My thanks to my fellow volunteers for their insight and advice, and, of course, thanks to the dogs who have taught me more than I can say.

Acknowledgments

For their technical advice and assistance, and for their dedication to excellence in their field, the author wishes to thank the following:

John Ard, Greyhound trainer, formerly of Seabrook Greyhound Park, New Hampshire

Lou Batdorf, Greyhound Pets of America representative, Wheeling, West Virginia

The Greyhound Project: Joan Belle Isle, Joan Dillon and Joan Martin, Milton, Massachussetts

Phil Hurst, operations manager, J. C. Ehrlich Co., Doylestown, Pennsylvania

Dr. Alan Klide, associate professor of veterinary anesthesia, University of Pennsylvania School of Veterinary Medicine

Christine Makepeace, REGAP director, Seabrook Greyhound Park, New Hampshire

Charlotte Mosner, Reynolds Greyhound Enterprises, Atlantic Beach, New York

Susan Netboy, Greyhound Friends for Life, Woodside, California

Dick Quackenbush, owner of Hay Hill Kennels, Green Brook, New Jersey

Love and gratitude to:

My parents, Elizabeth and Francis Branigan, who always encouraged my interest in animals and writing,

Cleveland Amory, who helped show me the way,

And my husband Charles Rissel, who helps me keep my sanity and makes so many things possible.

And a "thank you" just for being there to:

Ajax, George Banks, Betty Branigan, Bridget, Britannica, Tom Bruno, Bobby and Paddy Clancy, Vance Cole, Cheryl and Stephen Evans, Fiona, Charlie and Gary Ford, Owen Glendower, Annette and Fritz Goccia, Hamish, Lotus, Sheryl and Jay Leeb,

Bev and Roland Mostovy, Otis, Paco, Padillac, Marian Probst, Shaka, Daniel Stern, Jean Turoci, William Wallace and all the hardworking volunteers of Make Peace With Animals.

Vaya con Dios! to the great souls who have passed on:

Alice, Jean Boone, Alan Gray Branigan, Francis Branigan, Calvin, Clawdia, Conor, Duncan, Faisel, George, Giza, Gunsmoke, Harry, Hi Yo, Holly, Elvira Kaelin Hughes, Lydia Fels, Jasper, Monica Joyce, Judy, Kareem, Maggie, Mascara, Misty, Pennywise, Ramsey, Roberta, Betty Rosen, Roy, Rumi, Catherine Hume Schwartz, Seamus, Shana, Shooter, John Stephenson, Saul Stern, Stockbridge, Tasha, and Zula.

A special thanks to Sean Frawley, President of Howell Book House, who shares my enthusiasm for Greyhounds and who backed my idea for this book, and to my editor, Madelyn Larsen, who understands sighthounds and whose criticism of this book improved it greatly.

Introduction

When people harbor misconceptions about retired racing Greyhounds, they generally hold one of the following: that the dogs are old pensioners with at best only a year or so left of life, or that they as a breed are suited only for racing.

I'm happy to report that neither is true.

Until recently, when racing Greyhounds were finished with their careers, the fate met by many was euthanasia or sale to research laboratories. Now, thanks to the efforts of adoption centers across the country, these dogs are finally having their day.

Former racing Greyhounds are, in many important ways, unlike other dogs. Even seasoned dog owners may find some of their behavior baffling. Psychologically, physiologically and even historically, these dogs are different. Consequently, methods of training and care need to be adapted to fit their special needs. It is not that they are more difficult—quite the contrary—but they are unique. If you follow the advice in this book, all of which is based on extensive research and a good deal of personal experience, you will be able to help them fit in with ease.

Most Greyhounds available for adoption range in age from two to five years. Given that their life span is estimated at twelve to fourteen years, you can well expect to have a long and happy time with your ex-racer.

Racing is both highly competitive and physically demanding. Many young dogs may seem, to you, to be faster than the speed of light. But, compared to others of their breed, they don't quite measure up. These "slow" dogs, not much more than pups, may be sidelined almost before their careers begin. Other dogs may have suffered a minor injury on the track. While it probably doesn't affect them at all as a companion, it may have be enough to slow them down. In a sport where every second counts, this, too, may be a reason for retirement. Finally, there are the dogs that had a full racing career. By the age of five, most Greyhounds—even the superstars—have run out of steam. But, again, nearly two-thirds of their life is still ahead of them, and after all their hard work they, perhaps above all others, deserve a good retirement.

Greyhounds have, for thousands of years, been bred to do two things: run like the wind and work together with other dogs. They were not bred to be solitary hunters, and the transition from hunting to racing has kept the spirit of cooperation intact. For this reason, Greyhounds tend to get along with other dogs. Yet the muzzles worn by the racers cause some to infer that they are fighters. Not so. In Greyhound racing the dog whose nose crosses the finish line first is the winner. The muzzle helps make the nose more prominent and assists the judges in determining which dog won.

Of course, there is a safety factor involved. Whenever you have eight dogs, of any breed, in hot pursuit of something, be it a ball or an artificial rabbit, their natural desire to get the prize can cause the mildest dog to become competitive. But, once the object of their desire is removed, almost like magic they become their sweet old selves again.

Greyhounds are extremely companionable, good-natured dogs. In fact, as a breed, they seem to have a higher-than-average incidence of smiling. When they are very happy, such as when you get home, or when they want to play, many raise their upper lip and show their teeth. This is accompanied by wild tail-wagging and prancing. Who among us can resist such a goofy display?

There are two types of people for whom a retired racing Greyhound is ideal: those with families and those without. Let me explain.

Greyhounds, especially young males, have a great deal of patience, and most seem to understand that small children must be handled with care. If the playing gets too rough, Greyhounds tend to walk away rather than snap. Of course, children should always be supervised when playing with any dog and must be taught to respect the animal's feelings. But, as many families can attest, Greyhounds and gentle children are perfect together.

And for singles who are looking for an affectionate, loving pet, a Greyhound can't be beat. You will be rewarded many times over for whatever attention you give your dog. Greyhounds, perhaps because of their long and aristocratic history, are "to the manor born." They thrive in a home environment and take to it as if they waited all their lives for the experience. They are the sort of dog that likes keeping you within sight and have been known to follow their "person" from room to room.

In 1930, the British dog writer James Matheson praised the retired racer as a companion. He said of him, "His intelligence defies all attempts at description. There would appear to be nothing which he does not understand either in word or in gesture or the shadow of coming events. When your favourite has done his work, cherish him and give him a place with yourself for the rest of his but too short life. It is his one drawback. He should live as long as his owner."

By choosing to share your home and life with a Greyhound, you are participating in an act nearly as old as civilization itself. These are the same dogs that slept alongside the pharaohs, hunted with the noblemen of the Middle Ages, and have inspired artists and poets for thousands of years. Without a doubt they are worthy of us. The question is, are we worthy of them?

Chapter One

A Brief History of the Breed

ost dog-care books devote a page, or at most two, to the history of the breed they are discussing. There's a very good reason for this: there isn't that much history to tell. Greyhounds, however, have been with us longer than any other purebred dog. To appreciate fully your dog of today, it is useful to see him in a historical context. What follows is a brief outline to whet your appetite. For a more detailed look at the Greyhound's long and rich history, you might enjoy another book I've written—*The Reign of the Greyhound: A Popular History of the Oldest Family of Dogs* (Howell Book House, 1997).

THE GREYHOUND FAMILY

When contemplating the history of the Greyhound, it is useful to think in terms of the Greyhound family. As much as anyone may tell you that this or that breed is the oldest known to man, the truth is no one knows for sure. What we do know, however, is that the earliest purebred dogs were of the Greyhound type. The Greyhound family has several characteristics in common. Among them are long legs, a long narrow head, a deep chest and the ability to hunt by sight (hence the term *sighthound,* or *gazehound*) rather than by scent as most dogs do. As this type of dog moved to different parts of the world, some of his superficial characteristics, such as the length of his coat and the shape of his ears, began to change to accommodate the conditions of his new environment.

MEMBERS OF THE FAMILY

Members of the Greyhound family that are recognized by the American Kennel Club are Afghan Hounds, Borzois, Greyhounds, Ibizan Hounds, Irish Wolfhounds, Pharaoh Hounds, Salukis, Scottish Deerhounds and Whippets. Fringe members include Basenjis and Rhodesian Ridgebacks (which hunt by sight but do not share a physical resemblance) and Italian Greyhounds (which share a physical resemblance but don't hunt at all).

The musculature of a Greyhound.

THE FIRST GREYHOUND TYPES

The first traces of the long, lean dogs of the Greyhound type were seen in the ancient city of Catal-Hüyük, located in what is now southwest Turkey. Temple drawings, dating to 6000 B.C., show a hunter pursuing a stag with the help of two Greyhound types.

As people migrated to different parts of the globe, they took their dogs with them. About 4000 B.C., in what is now Iran, a funerary vase was created that was decorated with the image of Greyhounds. Obviously these dogs were held in high regard for their image to have been added to so personal an item.

ANCIENT EGYPT

It was in Egypt, however, that the Greyhound really came into his own. Not only were the dogs kept as companions (in addition to being hunting partners), but they were practically worshipped.

The Egyptian god Anubis was, as were many Egyptian deities, half man and half beast. In this case the beast was, depending on which sources you consult, either a jackal or a Greyhound. In looking at a painting or statue of Anubis, the resemblance to the present-day Pharaoh Hound is unmistakable.

The Egyptians valued their Greyhounds so much that the birth of one was second in importance only to the birth of a human boy. Indeed, when a pet Greyhound died, the entire family would mourn by shaving their heads, fasting and wailing.

Greyhounds were mummified and buried along with their owners, and the walls of the tombs were often decorated with figures of favorite Greyhounds that had died before their owners. Among the Pharaohs who kept Greyhounds were Tutankhamen, Amenhotep II, Thutmose III and Queen Hatshepsut. Cleopatra, too, was an aficionada.

While the ancient Israelites did not worship Greyhounds and, in fact, seemed to regard dogs in general with disdain, they did make an exception for the Greyhound. It is the only breed of dog named in the Bible. Proverbs 30: 29–31 reads:

The Egyptian god Anubis.

There be three things which go well, yea,
Which are comely in going:
A lion, which is strongest among beasts and
Turneth not away from any;
A Greyhound;
A he-goat also.

ANCIENT GREECE

When explorers from Greece traveled to Egypt, they were suitably impressed by the Greyhounds and managed to take some

7

back with them to their homeland. The dogs' popularity caught on to such an extent that even the Greek hero Alexander the Great kept one, which he named Peritas.

The first dog mentioned in literature, in 800 B.C., was, you guessed it, a Greyhound. In the Odyssey, Homer told the tale of the return of Odysseus, who had been away from home for twenty years. The only one who recognized him was his Greyhound, Argus, who was only a pup when Odysseus left.

Greek mythological figures were frequently portrayed with Greyhounds. Hecate, goddess of wealth, is often shown accompanied by a Greyhound, as is Pollux, protector of the hunt. And, of course, the famous story of Actaeon and Artemis tells of the goddess taking revenge on Actaeon by turning him into a stag and setting her forty-eight Greyhounds on him.

ANCIENT ROME

The ancient Romans appropriated many things of value from Greek culture, and this included an appreciation of the Greyhound. Their gods and goddesses, too, had Greyhounds, and the most well-known story is of Diana, goddess of the hunt, who gave her best friend, Procris, a Greyhound named Lelaps. Lelaps accompanied a hunter into the woods and, when the dog spotted a hare, went off in hot pursuit. The gods watched the scene and, not wanting the hare to be killed, turned both it and Lelaps into stone. This scene of Lelaps chasing the hare is often depicted in Roman art.

The Romans loved to run their Greyhounds, but in even those bloodthirsty days, there was at least one person who had a vestige of humanity. In A.D. 124 Arrian wrote a treatise entitled "On Hunting Hares." He urged his readers to concentrate more on the sport and less on the gore, stating, "The true sportsman does not take out his dogs to destroy the hares, but for the sake of the course and the contest between the dogs and the hares, and is glad if the hares escape."

MEDIEVAL AND RENAISSANCE TIMES

During the Middle Ages, a time of famine and pestilence, Greyhounds very nearly became extinct. They were saved, however, by clergymen who protected them from starvation and bred them for noblemen. It was during this period that ownership of a Greyhound became the exclusive right of the nobility.

King Canute enacted a law in 1016 in England that prohibited any "meane person" from owning a Greyhound and punished any infraction severely. A hundred years earlier in Wales, King Howel decreed the punishment for killing a Greyhound was the same as for killing a person—death.

Since Greyhounds were the first breed of dog mentioned in literature, it is only fitting that they also were the first breed of dog written about in the English language. In the late fourteenth century, Geoffrey Chaucer wrote in *The Canterbury Tales,* "Greyhounds he hadde as swift as fowels in flight." Shakespeare, too, mentioned them. In *Henry V* he wrote, "I see you stand like

A Greyhound head by the Italian Renaissance artist Pisanello, circa 1400.

Greyhounds in the slips, / [Straining] upon the start. The game's afoot!"

During the Renaissance, the elegant lines of the Greyhound were not overlooked by the most famous artists of the era. Among those who saw fit to immortalize these dogs in art were Veronese, Pisanello and Uccello. While Veronese's works tended toward the sacred, Pisanello and Uccello seemed to appreciate the Greyhound form for its own sake. Uccello's painting "Hunt in the Forest," for example, shows dozens of Greyhounds in a dark woods helping hunters capture their prey.

COURSING

The sport of coursing, which has its origins in ancient Greece, helped keep the Greyhound a popular animal. As coursing was originally practiced, two Greyhounds would be "slipped" (released) in a field to run after a hare that also would be released but given a hundred-yard advantage. The victor was not necessarily the dog that caught the rabbit, and, in fact, quite often the rabbit escaped. Instead, the dogs were judged by a complicated set of rules that valued such things as the dog's agility and

A modern Greyhound head shows very little change.

*Two famous coursing Greyhounds, Riot and David,
from an 1878 engraving.*

concentration. In the mid-1700s, a set of rules was developed that helped popularize the sport and caused it to spread throughout Great Britain and across the Continent.

THE BULLDOG BREEDINGS

The mid-1700s were also important in Greyhound history for another reason: it was then that an eccentric English nobleman by the name of Lord Orford began his now-famous Greyhound-Bulldog breedings. His idea was that by breeding a male Bulldog

11

Hecate was a second-generation cross from the Bulldog breedings of Lord Orford in the mid-1700s.

with a female Greyhound, the result would be a dog that had a uniformly smooth coat (which had eluded breeders up until that time) and which would possess what Lord Orford called "courage." Bear in mind, however, that the Bulldogs of those times did not look like the Bulldogs of today. They had a much longer muzzle and resembled Bull Terriers.

Lord Orford's crosses continued for seven generations, and the resulting dogs were of such high quality that those who had previously been skeptical were now clamoring to buy his dogs.

ON TO AMERICA

As people from the British Isles emigrated to America, they often brought their Greyhounds with them. Coursing was a sport that was a natural for the wide-open expanses of the prairie, and the participants justified the killing of rabbits with the argument that they were helping to protect the farmers' crops from hungry hares. General George Custer coursed his fourteen Greyhounds on the day before his defeat at Little Big Horn. Perhaps he had a premonition about the next day's battle because directly after coursing his dogs, he sent them off with an officer into town so they would stay out of harm's way.

Greyhound Racing . . . an American Sport

In the early 1900s, Owen Patrick Smith invented the artificial lure that accomplished two things at once: it allowed more people to see the Greyhounds as they were raced on an oval track, and it eliminated the need to kill live rabbits. And so, Greyhound racing was born. In the years since, Greyhound racing has become increasingly popular. It reached its peak in 1991 when it was the sixth most popular spectator sport, with revenues of $3.4 billion from betting. Casino gambling has sharply cut into Greyhound racing's popularity, and profitability, but it is still a major industry. In 1995 the total betting revenue was $2.5 billion.

But the history of the Greyhound is not finished yet. The one you write with your dog will be the most interesting of all.

Greyhound racing is a sport made in the United States.
(Photo: National Greyhound Association)

Chapter Two

Choosing the Right Dog for You

*O*ne of the most important things you can do to foster a good relationship with your dog should take place before you even get him: choosing in advance the right dog for you.

How, you ask, can this be done in advance? Simple. Make a list of all the desirable traits you would like your dog to have. And if a specific color is at the top of that list, you're in trouble before you even begin.

Let me explain . . .

People who adopt ex-racers usually do so by one of two methods: either they travel to a kennel that houses retired dogs, or they adopt through an organization that gets a dog for them. Both methods can be perfectly suitable or fraught with peril. Adopting a dog is a serious commitment and is a decision you may live with for ten to fifteen years. It is definitely not to be entered into on a whim nor for a superficial consideration such as the dog's color. This is why I recommend a list because it can help make it clear to you exactly what you are looking for in a dog and why.

SHOULD YOU HAVE A DOG?

First, you need to give serious thought to whether or not you are ready for the responsibility of *any* dog. If you work very long hours and live in a small apartment, a cat or bird may be a better companion. Remember, too, that there is more to owning a dog than simply feeding him twice a day. Dogs need exercise, training, grooming, regular veterinary care, and lots of affection. Can you afford all of this in both time and money?

WHY DO YOU WANT A GREYHOUND?

Now ask yourself why, specifically, you want a Greyhound. Perhaps you have been caught up in the plight of the ex-racers and want to help. Helping is admirable, of course, but is adopting a Greyhound really the best way for you to assist? It's possible that you could serve the cause better by finding other people who want to adopt. Another possibility is to provide a foster home for a Greyhound. That way you can provide a much-needed service for the adoption agency and get an idea of what it would be like to have one in your home. Who knows—you may wind up adopting the foster dog yourself!

There are three things about Greyhounds that may cause people to want another breed: they are large dogs, they can never be allowed to run off-lead except in fenced areas and they are not good watchdogs.

DO YOU HAVE ENOUGH SPACE?

As to the first point, even though I tell people that Greyhounds are small large dogs (rather like the seeming contradiction of the name Little Big Horn), what I mean by that is that they are graceful, short-coated and often curl up in a tight ball when they sleep. Because of that they don't have as much of a physical presence as, say, a Newfoundland or a St. Bernard. They are, however, undeniably bigger than a Chihuahua or any of the many medium-sized breeds. Do you have the space for those long legs, or will you and the Greyhound constantly be tripping over each other?

WHY GREYHOUNDS CANNOT RUN LOOSE

The second point of not letting the dog run free pretty well speaks for itself, but there are so many people who adopt who think that their dog is somehow different and can be trusted not to run away. Let me support the statement with some facts and a few sad anecdotes.

Greyhounds are among the fastest land mammals, with speeds reaching 41.72 mph. Horses, by comparison, have been known to reach 43.26 mph. If you think that you will simply run and catch your Greyhound if he bolts, consider this: a sprinting man can run only 27.89 mph. Therefore, catching a running Greyhound is only slightly less difficult than catching a running horse— which is to say, impossible.

Greyhounds have been bred for literally thousands of years for one thing: speed. If you think an obedience course is enough to wipe out eons of genetics and training, you are deluding yourself *and* risking your dog's life. In the case of retired racers, the situation is more acute because they have had the speed/chase mentality reinforced in them from the moment they were born. And, as we all know, what we learn as a child (or puppy) is what tends to stay with us for life.

Even before I began placing retired racers, I was drawn to them for their beauty and serenity. Every October I travel to New York City to attend the Feast of St. Francis at the Cathedral of St. John the Divine. On that day, all animals, from the huge elephant in the procession to the household pet, are welcome inside the church. The entire service is devoted to a celebration of animal life.

Every year I used to talk to a man who came all the way from Boston for the event with his two beautiful ex-racers. The dogs were so calm and loving that they would try to sit on his lap in the pew! Last year he came with only one dog. When I inquired about the other I heard the answer I feared: the dog was dead.

Despite warnings from the person he had adopted the dogs from, the man felt he knew his dogs well enough and had lived with them long enough (five years) that the advice to keep them on a lead no longer applied. Besides, he reasoned, the dogs had been obedience-trained. So, for several years he had been allowing them to run free in a large park in Boston well away from the park's boundaries. His version of Russian roulette worked quite well until that fateful day when a squirrel crossed the Greyhound's path. Perhaps the dog felt especially good that day. Perhaps some old chasing memory clicked inside his brain. For whatever reason, he took off and ignored the call of his owner. The boundary of the park meant nothing to the dog, and we can only hope that when he ran between two parked cars and into the path of a bus that his death was swift and painless.

Here's another tale, which, while obviously foolhardy, gives you another idea of what can happen:

A woman from Florida who had adopted a Greyhound almost a year earlier took her dog, unleashed, to a Fourth of July parade. Naturally there were crowds, the sounds of marching bands, and the occasional firecracker. It was a firecracker that so startled the otherwise calm dog that he took off. Several people tried to catch him, but his fear exceeded their speed. His dead body, obviously hit by a car, was found the next day ten miles from the parade site.

So, if you adopt a Greyhound, are you willing to keep him leashed? He can run in your fenced yard, of course. And if you don't have a fenced yard, perhaps you have a friend or neighbor who would let you release your dog once or twice a week in their yard. Another alternative is a fully enclosed tennis court, football or baseball field. If none of the above is available, let me assure you that a good brisk walk once or twice a day will more than satisfy your dog's exercise needs.

GREYHOUNDS ARE COMPANIONS, NOT GUARD DOGS

If you are looking for a dog that will do double duty as both a pet and a protector, perhaps you should investigate other breeds.

Greyhounds are very unaggressive dogs, and the vast majority of them will not even bark when they see a stranger approaching the house. One of the remarks people often make after attending a gathering of Greyhounds is that the dogs are so quiet! They are watchdogs only in the sense that they will watch, but probably not act.

HOW TO CHOOSE YOUR IDEAL GREYHOUND

Now that you've decided that you do want a Greyhound, consider the following factors (listed in order of importance).

PERSONALITY

What type of personality would you like your dog to have?

While all Greyhounds share some traits in common, there are individual differences. Do you want an extremely affectionate dog? Some people find it charming when a dog follows them from room to room, others consider it an annoyance. Do you want a very intelligent dog? If you do, make sure you channel the energy into something constructive because brains left untrained can think up things to do that might not be pleasing to your sense of order. Do you want a very quiet dog? Companionable and low key to one person may add up to dull and boring to another.

ACTIVITY LEVEL

What sort of activity level do you desire in your dog? Very peppy? A potential jogging companion? A couch potato?

Be realistic. If you adopt a very athletic, active dog with the thought that it will somehow inspire you to exercise, think about what your own "track record" has been. Do you have a basement full of exercise equipment that was bought on a whim and rarely used since? Do you have a kitchen full of dust-covered diet drinks or an unused health club membership? A very active Greyhound is not going to be happy if his only exercise is

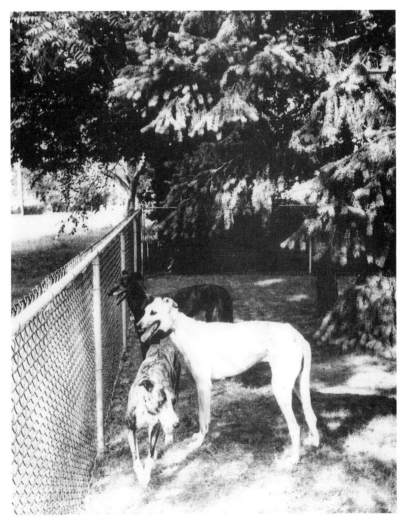

Maddie, Rumi and Leggs, safe in a fenced yard.

following you from the refrigerator to the recliner. If you are currently exercising regularly, then do, by all means, consider a Greyhound as a jogging companion. If, however, you expect him to inspire you, try the local gym first and see how long you stick with it.

Also, even if you are very active when you get home from work, but are gone from the house eight to ten hours a day, it is unrealistic to expect a very energetic dog to go into a state of suspended animation while you aren't around and then suddenly become a ball of fire the minute you step inside the door. Look for a dog that is injury-free but only moderately active. That way he'll be calm enough to doze off while you're gone, but able to do some long hikes or short jogs with you.

AGE

Do you have a preference as to the age of the dog?

Racing Greyhounds, because they had a relatively regimented early life, tend to mature emotionally somewhat slower than other dogs. For this reason, a two-year-old is often very much a puppy. Is that appealing to you, or would you prefer a dog that has already worked out such stages as chewing and jumping around? Also, remember that the life span of a Greyhound is from twelve to fourteen years. Try to imagine where you will be ten years from now. Perhaps you would be better off choosing a somewhat older dog. My experience has shown me that older dogs—from, say, five to six years—are even more grateful for their retirement homes and still have many good years ahead!

OTHER PETS

Do you have other pets? Does your ex-racer need to get along with your cats?

Generally speaking, other dogs are not a problem, but a small number of ex-racers see cats, birds and very little dogs as moving prey. Make sure you tell the adoption agency or the person running the kennel that your new dog must get along with your other pets. There can be no guarantees, of course, when you are dealing with animals, but the person in charge should be able to direct you to a dog that he or she is fairly certain will fit in with the rest of your family.

And, by the way, don't think that you will somehow train a dog out of the habit of lunging for cats. When the instinct is

Greyhound activity ranges from this . . .

. . . to this!

Ajax and Phoebe, an Airedale, in interbreed rapport.

deeply ingrained, the only homes for these few are ones without small pets. Some groups try electric shock collars to "deprogram" the dogs, but I find the method to be a cruel and extremely crude way to train. Don't try it! There are plenty of homes without small pets that are perfect for the dyed-in-the-wool chasers, so there's really no reason to force the issue!

Another thing to remember is that just because a dog is not small-animal friendly, it has no bearing on how he will be as a pet. I have known cat-safe Greyhounds that were indifferent to people, and Greyhounds that had a high prey drive yet were devoted family pets. It depends on the dog.

CHILDREN

Do you have children? If you do and they are very young, will your ex-racer need to have a lot of patience?

No dog is foolproof around kids, but some seem to enjoy the activity of children, while others would rather be left alone. As I said in the introduction, most Greyhounds are inherently kind, but you must not try their patience by allowing children to do whatever they want to them or any other pet. I am not only referring to children who are overtly aggressive with pets by doing such things as pulling their ears. I also mean children who are constantly falling over or stepping on the dog, or ones who will just never let the dog rest. Dogs can't tell whether something that is annoying them is intentional or accidental, and they really don't care. All they know is that it's a source of irritation.

My experience has been that young male Greyhounds have more tolerance for children than do the females. I believe the reason for this is that females tend to regard children as puppies. It is in their nature to discipline their own puppies when they get too boisterous, and some do the same with human children. This is usually evidenced by growling or barking when their patience has been pushed to the limit. Males, on the other hand, tend to see children as siblings. Males play more actively, so a rough-and-tumble session is what they expect.

The presence of children or grandchildren in the home is a fact that you must reveal to the person handling the adoption. And if you are picking out the dog in person, by all means bring your children along so you can judge the dog's reaction to them.

King relaxing with friends Daniel, Clawdia (foreground) and Alice (background).

COMPANION OR PROTECTOR?

Are you looking just for a companion or for a companion and protector?

By nature Greyhounds are not aggressive animals, so, for guard duty, they are not ideal. There are some that will bark when a stranger approaches the house and that, coupled with their size, might be enough to deter someone with the idea of breaking in, but barkers are in the distinct minority. In big cities where there tend to be more guard dogs, I have noticed people watching me and my dog approach them on the street and actually crossing to the other side as we get close, and then crossing back again after we pass. This is amusing because my dogs look to me for protection! From adopting out these dogs I have had more than a few people tell me that they are afraid of black dogs (I personally find them to be the most beautiful). So, if you want a dog that commands respect, you might consider a black one, but please remember that they are, in fact, no more aggressive than dogs of any other color.

SIZE

Is size a consideration?

Think about the size of your house, your yard and even your car. The smallest female can weigh as little as the mid-forties. The largest male can reach the mid-nineties. Both cases are rare. Generally the females range from 50 to 60 pounds and the males from 65 to 75 pounds. Obviously a Greyhound, even a relatively small one, is going to take up more room than, say, a Fox Terrier. The largest male we ever placed was Conor, whose racing weight was 105 pounds. The smallest female was Wee Wicked, whose weight was 40 pounds. Both dogs represent the extreme, not the average. Greyhounds are, however, graceful dogs that seem to know how to tuck themselves into small spaces. Most people who see a Greyhound for the first time consider them huge, but after a while they get used to their size and realize that Greyhounds are basically all legs!

Fiona demonstrates how Greyhounds can tuck into small spaces.

GENDER

Do you have a preference as to the gender of the dog?

Because there are already more Greyhounds than there are homes for them, responsible adoption agencies will either require you to spay or neuter your new dog, or they will have it done in advance. If altering the dog is up to you, bear in mind that it is less expensive to neuter a male than it is to spay a female. And, in case you were wondering, adult male Greyhounds are not more aloof than the females and are every bit as affectionate! The only difference between a neutered male and a spayed female is that, in most cases, the males are larger. Beyond that, it's just a matter of personal preference.

If you already have a dog (either a Greyhound or any other breed) and you are planning to add a Greyhound to your family, it is generally a safe bet to have a male and female together. In

25

Sophie (left), a female, and Ajax (right), a male.

those cases, it is usually the female that becomes dominant. With two females together there is sometimes a bit of jockeying for position (the same can be true of two males), but it usually works out.

Don't believe what you've heard about male dogs not getting along. You can imagine that I pretty much have my choice of any dog, yet my present pack consists of four males and two females. The main thing to keep in mind is matching their temperaments. If they get along, then it doesn't matter what sex they are.

I am always astonished when people applying to adopt a Greyhound from me insist on a female because they are sure that males will urinate in the house. I am quick to point out that males are every bit as easy to housebreak as females. Furthermore, if a dog of either sex is soiling the house, it is the fault of the owner, not the dog. A housebroken dog may have an accident if he is under stress or brought into a new environment. But such a scenario could just as easily occur with a female as with a male. I'm sure my four "clean as wax" males would be mortally offended if they knew how their entire gender was being falsely accused!

COLOR

Do you have a color preference?

As I said in the beginning, looks should be your last consideration because, once the dog is yours, trust me, it will suddenly become the most beautiful dog in the world. There is a wide array of Greyhound colors including black, white, fawn (tan), cream, red (rust), many shades of brindle (striped) and white with either red, fawn, black or brindle patches. The one color you will rarely see is grey (called blue). Whether it is fact or fiction, the feeling in the racing world is that the blue dogs are not good

Three males in harmony: Ajax (front), Jasper (left) and King (right).

runners. For that reason they are seldom available for adoption after retirement because most never raced to begin with! Many in the racing world also feel that the blue dogs are prone to cancer and skin problems. Again, although I could find no facts to back up the prejudice against blue dogs, it is something to consider. After all, those within the industry have had lots of experience, and they should be in a position to know which dogs are the healthiest.

Again, keep in mind that you are adopting a dog to save his life. Would you really consider a dog less worthy of adoption, or less loveable, because of his color? If so, perhaps you should rethink your motivation for adoption.

FINANCIAL CONSIDERATIONS

Upon hearing of the plight of the Greyhound many people are moved to adopt one, or more, without any thought of what such a decision might cost them in the future. While the adoption fee may be minimal (depending on the agency from which you adopt), there are going to be veterinary and other expenses in your dog's future. Are you going to be able to afford to give a Greyhound proper care?

In terms of the adoption fee, you would do well to shop around. Most agencies operate on a volunteer basis. This does not mean that they have no expenses, it simply means that the workers donate their services to get you the dog you want. If you are dealing with an agency that either operates a kennel or has paid employees (or both), you can expect the adoption fee to reflect their added expenses.

All agencies have telephone and postage costs. Beyond that, and depending on the level of veterinary care the dog has received before adoption, you will be expected to reimburse the agency for those services. Many groups give a copy of this book with each adoption and, of course, they did not get the book for free. Some put a new safety collar with matching leash and an ID tag on the dog and give out other post-adoption materials. In my opinion, Greyhound adoptions should not be turned into a business. The dogs have already been part of a money-making operation, and the retirement part of their lives should be free of such considerations. Make sure that the group you are adopting from has the dog's best interests at heart and that they are not just trying to "make a sale" or to inflate grossly the cost of services they received either for free or at minimal cost.

Beyond the adoption fee, you must think of dog-related expenses in the long term. As they say, things happen. While the vast majority of ex-racers are very healthy, there is the chance that yours may develop a health condition or have an accident in the future. If you are barely able to meet your own expenses, will you be able to pay for, let's say, expensive surgery or costly diagnostic tests? Quite apart from that, what about yearly check-ups and inoculations? How about flea and tick control? Regular toenail trimming? Good quality food? A warm coat for the winter? Be honest with yourself. If you know that you may fall short, then consider helping the local adoption group instead, and put off your own adoption until you can do it right.

ADOPTING A GREYHOUND

There are innumerable ways in which to adopt a Greyhound. As was mentioned earlier, the two methods that are most common are visiting a kennel of retired racers or having an agency choose for you. Either method is fine as long as you stick to your list of requirements.

If you visit a kennel, the people there ought to be in a position to do two things to help the adoption along. First, they should be able to direct you toward dogs that match what you are looking for. Because they take care of the dogs, they are likely to be familiar with each dog's temperament. Second, they may be able to give you an idea of the dog's history, and, with any luck, his medical history.

As to the first point, tell the person in charge exactly what you want. If he or she seems to disregard your request and attempts to push a wild-eyed youngster on you when you specifically stated that you wanted a companion for your retirement years, ask to speak to someone else.

I might as well warn you right now that when it comes time to make a decision, it will be hard. Nothing is more appealing than the soulful look in a Greyhound's eyes staring at you from behind the wire mesh of a crate. My advice? Stand firm and remember what you are looking for. Several visits may be appropriate, as it will get you used to the kennel setting and it will give you a chance to think over the dogs that were "contenders" during your first visit.

As to the second point, it can be useful to know your dog's medical history as well as his racing record, but for some dogs a medical history may be nonexistent. Not all trainers are good record keepers. Many dogs, for example, receive their yearly inoculations but no records are kept. Some adopters mistakenly assume that trainers keep a "baby book" of each dog's first training session or first winning race. The fact is that many records are kept in the trainer's head. When time is short and staffing is

Will you be able to resist the pleading eyes of a Greyhound that needs a home?

inadequate, many kennels concentrate on the most immediate demands on their time—namely, feeding, cleaning up and training. Record keeping under these circumstances can become a luxury. Adoption groups always request medical histories, but they do not always receive them. If this turns out to be the case with the dog you have selected, then you should at least receive the latest inoculation record. And, as with choosing any dog, look for clear eyes, a clean nose and no obvious signs of illness or injury.

Broken legs, broken toes and pulled ligaments are not uncommon injuries in the racing world. Some dogs recover fully from such ailments, while others may be left with a limp ranging from slight to pronounced. Some injuries can be corrected by surgery. If such a handicap is a minor flaw to you, then I encourage you to select one of these deserving Greyhounds, as most potential adopters, and, sadly, many adoption groups, will overlook dogs with any defects.

If you are choosing a female, try to find out if she was on hormones to prevent her heat cycle, and, if she was, for how long. If she wasn't, find out when she had her last heat. As with medical records, this sort of information is not always available. Unless you are told otherwise, assume that a female was on hormones and that, once off, she could go into heat at any time (although, in a minority of cases, females who have been on hormones never go into heat again). It is not at all uncommon, when we take in a shipment of dogs, for a female to go into heat in the truck on her way to us. When one female goes into heat, it is also common for the other females on board to follow suit. When that is the case, you must wait for about a month after the bleeding has subsided to have her spayed.

Of course you need to know if the dog has already been spayed or, in the case of males, neutered and, if so, when. It is estimated that it takes thirty days for the hormone level in a dog's body to adjust to being altered, so, especially in the case of males, allow for some of the more typical male behavior to subside gradually after neutering.

Other questions to ask are how recently the dog was retired as well as why he was retired. If he was retired because of an injury, find out what kind. This is especially important if you plan on participating in certain sports with the dog, such as artificial lure coursing. The dog may be in perfect health, but some injuries may preclude certain activities. If you are simply planning to nurture a house pet, don't let a minor racing injury bother you. Most will never affect a dog that simply takes walks with his owner or even one that races around the backyard. But, if you are planning vigorous exercise with your Greyhound, tell the adoption person in advance.

One other point concerning the racing career is how well the dog did on the track. Often a dog that did extremely well is treated differently (better) than the other dogs. This will sometimes affect the dog's behavior in retirement.

Take the case of Amber. While she was in the foster home awaiting adoption, she literally took over the house. She demanded to be the first one fed, she took everyone's toys away from them and she snatched the softest bed away from one of the long-time residents. When, on the rare occasion that she was reprimanded, she pouted for hours afterward. It was quite unusual for a new dog to be so bossy, but when we discovered that she had been a champion at the track as well as the trainer's favorite, suddenly it all made sense. She was spoiled, plain and simple!

If you are choosing sight unseen, you may actually be at an advantage. This way you won't be at the mercy of all those soulful eyes. It is essential, however, that the adoption agency knows what you want and can be trusted to get it. Faults in judgment do occur, of course, and sometimes a dog can behave one way in the kennel and quite differently in a home, but try to make sure that the agency is really trying for a match and not just a placement. Make sure, too, that they are willing to take back, or exchange, a dog that just does not fit in with your lifestyle.

It is hard to generalize about what you are likely to encounter with a new dog off the track. The first thing that comes to mind, however, is a bald bottom. Many of them have had the hair worn off the back and sides of their legs from rubbing against the walls of the crates they are housed in. This is nothing to worry about. Most dogs start growing hair back within a few weeks. In some cases, hair loss is suggestive of an underactive thyroid. But, before jumping to that conclusion, read the thyroid material in Chapter Five so you will know exactly what type of test to have your veterinarian perform. It is extremely unwise to begin thyroid therapy based on an assumption.

Another thing that is sometimes seen is skin irritation on the chest. This is caused by blocked pores (blackheads)—the result of dogs lying in the sand of the turnout pen. The problem can be treated easily by applying warm compresses to the area then gently squeezing the clogged pores or by applying an ointment from your vet. You can, of course, leave it alone, as it causes no pain to the dog.

Occasionally we will see a dog fresh off of the track with one or both elbows swollen. The swelling resembles a golf ball under the skin. The cause of this condition is inadequate bedding, and the best treatment we have found is to just leave it alone. In three to four weeks time the swelling subsides and the dog once again has a normal appearance. We have known of veterinarians who have attempted to aspirate the fluid, and in every case, the condition has worsened. Yes, the swelling is unsightly. No, it is not painful, so if you just have patience and give the dog plenty of bedding, the swelling should go away on its own.

People sometimes erroneously assume that a dog with scars is a fighter. This is probably not the case. After all, racing Greyhounds are muzzled almost all the time. Scars can be the result of a pile-up on the track or even the result of a loose wire on a fence or on the door of their crate. Even if the scars were the result of a fight, which is most unlikely, remember that it is generally the victim that winds up with scars, not the aggressor.

As for personality testing, the best recommendation I can give is to opt for a dog with a moderate personality. Choose neither the most active nor the most subdued. Sometimes the overly

Typical baldness from crate rubbing at the track.

active dog can be too much to handle for the average owner. Likewise, the overly subdued, submissive type can become panic-stricken when frightened (and it often doesn't take much to get a dog in that state). A simple, mild-mannered, uncomplicated dog generally makes the best pet.

Choose a dog with your head and heart.

A Greyhound will reward you with never-ending affection . . .

. . . and will be your best friend.

FOLLOW YOUR HEAD AND HEART

Now that you have the ideal Greyhound (for you) in mind, here's a little advice that may seem contradictory to all I've said so far: be flexible. Try to get the most important qualities you are looking for, but if one dog catches your eye and you make a connection, give the dog a chance. Perhaps the dog is a little smaller than you wanted, and maybe he doesn't seem quite as smart, but there is a lot to be said for the chemistry that sometimes occurs between a person and a dog. Go with your head and heart.

Chapter Three

The Racing Life

*J*n order to understand fully why your ex-racer acts the way he does, it is helpful to know where he came from and how he is used to living life. Many of his current habits are the direct result of years of training. Knowing why he does something can assist you in changing any of his behavior that you find undesirable or in reinforcing good behavior.

THE BUSINESS ARRANGEMENTS

Racing kennels are often, but not always, located in a compound on the grounds of the Greyhound racetrack. Each kennel is owned by a different person who, in most cases, hires a trainer. The kennel owners are responsible for all the bills (food, veterinary fees and so on) that a dog incurs and for paying wages to the trainer and kennel helpers. The trainer is responsible for training a dog and for deciding which races a dog will enter and when. The owners pay nothing toward a dog's maintenance at the track, but when a dog earns money, a standard arrangement is that the kennel owner gets 65 percent of the winnings (5 percent of which is paid to the trainer), while the owner gets 35 percent. In a typical kennel, dogs from many different owners are housed and trained together.

Many owners own lots of different dogs and can have them under contract to kennels all over the country. Likewise, many owners never even meet their dogs. They can buy and sell their racers over the phone.

To a great extent, owners of a racing dog must rely on trust in the kennel owner and trainer. Often they take the trainer's word for it when they are advised to buy or sell a dog. They also must trust the kennel owner to provide proper veterinary care and nutrition for the dog. In the majority of cases, the trainers treat

Golly Wally communes with his trainer, Louis Palazzo.

the dogs well in the hopes that the dogs will, in turn, perform well on the track.

THE DAILY ROUTINE

Racing kennels consist of double-deck banks of crates along the inside walls of the building with an aisle down the middle. Standard crate size is $2^1/_2$ feet wide, 3 feet high and $3^1/_2$ feet deep.

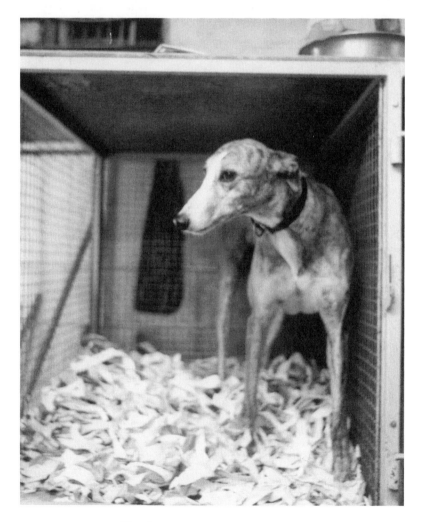

Jill in her crate at the adoption kennel.

Chris Makepeace turning out the female Greyhounds.
The males are on the other side of the fence.

The preferred bedding is shredded newspaper, since it provides both insulation and a deep cushion. Both are very important, as Greyhounds, which have very little hair and virtually no fat to act as padding, are easily chilled and prone to pressure sores when exposed to hard surfaces.

The day begins early at the track, and the same routine is repeated without variation. Generally the dogs are turned out for the first time at 6 or 6:30 in the morning. Three more turnouts follow in a day: 10 A.M., 4 P.M. and 9 P.M. The turnout pen is divided into two sides, one for the males and one for the females. The dogs are always turned out with their muzzles on to prevent any confrontations. As will be described in detail in Chapter Seven, "Training," these are not their racing muzzles but, rather, a smaller, lighter type used solely for turn-out and traveling.

While the dogs are relieving themselves and stretching their legs, the trainers and their helpers are busy cleaning any of the crates that have been soiled during the night. Most Greyhounds do not soil their crates, but accidents do happen.

THE HANDLING OF THE DOGS

When the dogs are brought in, perhaps thirty to forty minutes later, each one is checked before being put back into the crate. The average kennel houses about forty dogs (although there can be as many as seventy-five to one hundred), and the trainer must know each one. The length and condition of their toenails and pads are checked, their eyes and ears are examined and, by lifting the dog into the crate and giving it the once-over, the trainer can tell if a dog is getting enough or too much to eat. Because of these frequent examinations, Greyhounds are used to being handled. Even as pups on the farm they are handled daily for such things as weighing, deworming, or being led to the turn-out pen.

THEIR MUSICAL BACKGROUND

One constant I have observed in every racing kennel is the sound of music—nonstop, twenty-four hours a day. I personally found it a bit maddening (especially some of the radio stations chosen), but I suppose you can get used to anything after a while. It was

Typical arrangement of crates; turnout muzzles, made of lightweight wire or plastic, hang on doors.

explained to me that the music serves two purposes. First, it calms the dogs and provides yet another constant in their life. Second, it helps drown out noises from the outside. If, for example, a truck pulled up during the night, all of the dogs would assume they were about to be turned out and would get up and bark. Pretty soon the entire racing compound would be awake and barking. Racing dogs need their rest, so, as strange as it may seem, the music is always on.

FEEDING

Food is extremely important in a racing kennel, both in quantity and quality. Racing Greyhounds have what is known as a set weight, which is basically the weight at which they look good and run well. Maintaining that weight is an art and a science, and there are as many different opinions on how to achieve it as there are racing kennels.

Dogs are not fed the day they are raced. A dog is not permitted to run on a full stomach because it can cause gastric torsion. Instead, dogs are given a few biscuits to tide them over until after the race.

TRAINING

By the time a dog has reached racing age, at approximately seventeen months, he has already had a good deal of training. Some of it came naturally, some was man-made.

Most racing Greyhounds are born on farms in the Midwest and in Florida. Bitches that have been bred are kept in special brooding kennels away from the other dogs. A few hours before she gives birth, the bitch makes an elaborate nest in her brooding box. Greyhounds are known for their keen maternal instincts, and rarely will a bitch reject her litter. Some bitches are still producing litters at ten to twelve years of age, although humane treatment would suggest an earlier retirement from motherhood. At birth, Greyhound puppies look like any other little dogs, and it is not until they are about three months of age that the distinctive long legs and long muzzle develop.

43

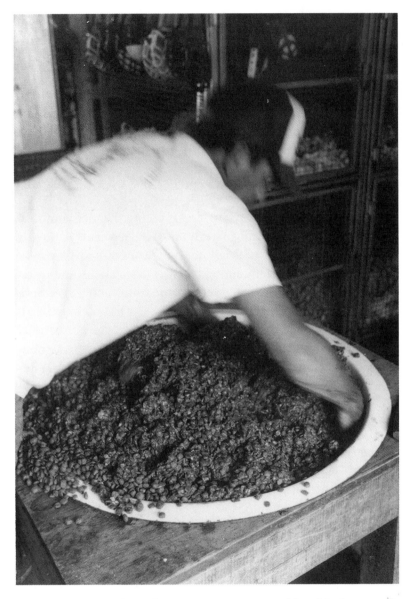

Trainer John Ard prepares enormous quantities of food.

The pups are weaned by their mothers when they are eight to nine weeks old. By that age, their teeth and claws are surprisingly sharp. Although the pups are separated from their mothers, they are not separated from each other. In fact, a litter of pups, which can range in number from one to sixteen, but averages six to eight, usually remains together until they are eight to ten months old. The reason for this, in part, is because the pups help to train each other. At weaning age their ears are tattooed, which identifies them for the racing business.

At commercial breeding farms, young pups are turned out in fenced runs that are 250 to 300 feet long. As young as two months, pups begin racing with each other up and down the length of the runs. In good weather they are out for twenty to thirty minutes at a time, and if you watch them closely, you can see them already competing with each other.

At six months of age their training begins in earnest. Most trainers start out by tying a plastic jug to a rope, pulling it along the ground and having the pups chase it. Later on, a jug or an animal pelt is pulled along by a slow-moving tractor. Still later the dogs run after an artificial lure suspended on a whirligig, and finally, they run in simulated racetrack conditions. Although it is illegal in most states to train the Greyhounds on a live lure, such as a rabbit, the practice still persists in some areas. Some old-time dog trainers swear that until a dog has tasted blood he's no good at the track. Of course, such cruel myths have no basis in fact, to which racing records will attest.

A Greyhound first gets a collar around his neck at four months of age. From the age of about eight months, Greyhounds learn to walk on a lead. The reasons for this early training are obvious: Their entire lives are spent being led from one place to another. With so many dogs to handle, a trainer cannot waste time with a dog that pulls or stops frequently. This training holds them in good stead when they become companions, too.

THEIR FIRST RACE

The first professional race a Greyhound competes in is called his maiden race. Maidens are reserved for dogs, males or females, that have never won a race before. Typically races have eight dogs, but occasionally there are nine. The average age at which a Greyhound runs his maiden race is eighteen months.

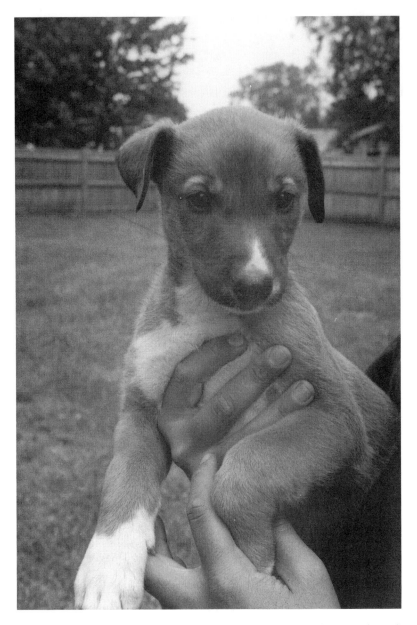

At nine weeks of age, a Greyhound pup doesn't look much like a Greyhound!

(Left to right) King (Low Key Two) and his littermate Tim (Counterpoint Two), shown here with turnout muzzles, both ran and won in Grade A at major tracks. (Photo: Charlotte Mosner)

Speed is not the only factor that determines which dog will win. A dog must possess endurance and agility, too. If a dog bursts from the starting box with all of his might and holds no energy in reserve, he may well finish last. A dog must also concentrate on the lure and, simultaneously, keep his eyes on the other dogs so he doesn't accidentally bump into them. A pileup on the track could result in serious injuries and, of course, slows everyone down. Finally, a dog must not be guilty of interference, which means that he must not purposely bump other dogs or start fights with them.

A young Greyhound is given six chances to come in first, second, third, or fourth in a maiden race. If he does not accomplish this, he is either "retired" and put up for adoption or is euthanized. I wonder how many of the betting public know that a young dog's very life can depend on whether he wins, places or shows in a race.

ASCENDING THE RANKS

Assuming that all goes well and that a dog finally wins a maiden race, he is then promoted to Grade J, which is for dogs that have just won the maiden. Other grades, from A to D, depend on how a dog places after each race he runs. Generally speaking, a dog gradually ascends the grades, then, as he ages and slows down, descends. The difference in speed, by the way, between a Grade-A dog and a Grade-D dog can be as little as $^3/_4$ of a second.

KEEPING RACING HONEST

Every dog that wins a race has his urine analyzed for the presence of illegal drugs. Forbidden substances include butazolidin (an anti-inflammatory), stimulants, depressants, steroids and even aspirin. Ninety-seven drugs can be detected by the tests, the object of which is to keep racing honest. In addition to the winner, one other dog is picked at random after each race to be tested.

Racing bitches are every bit as fast as the dogs. To prevent them from going into heat (which would not only slow them down but would cause the dogs to riot back at the kennel), they are given testosterone. When their racing careers are over and they are taken off the hormone, many females go into heat immediately while others never go into heat again (see Chapter Two, "Choosing the Right Dog for You").

Usually there are thirteen to fifteen races in a day, and an individual dog is run only once every three to four days. By the time a dog reaches the finish line he has burned up all the available carbohydrates in his body. R and R is greatly needed.

At the finish line the dogs, wearing no collars—only racing muzzles and numbered blankets—are caught by the person who led them onto the track and are handed over to someone from the dog's kennel. The dog is walked for a few minutes to cool down and is taken back to the kennel to rest and drink water. An hour or so after the race the dog is fed. In most kennels, a dog that has won is given a special treat. The ones that don't win are, literally, in the dog house.

RACING INJURIES

There are several hazards that a racing dog faces on the track. Some injuries can lead to retirement, while others can lead to death. When you consider the tremendous speeds that these dogs can reach, it is a wonder that broken legs are not more common. With luck, and proper veterinary care, a leg can be set and a dog can eventually resume racing. For others, though, a break can be so severe that they can never race again. Some injuries are caused by dogs bumping into each other and others are caused by unsafe track conditions. Perhaps the worst possible accident for dogs is electrocution from falling into the cradle that holds the electric lure. Thankfully, this is a relatively rare occurrence.

Other common injuries are torn ligaments, broken bones, pulled tendons, dislocated toes and various cuts, scrapes and bruises. One injury peculiar to Greyhound racing is known as a spike. Spikes occur by accident during the course of a race when the toenail of one dog punctures the back of the leg or foot of

Racing Greyhounds can reach speeds over 40 mph.
(Photo: National Greyhound Association)

another dog. If untreated the puncture can become infected, but, when treated properly, it is a minor, albeit painful, mishap.

A veterinarian is present at each race and is responsible for all the dogs that are running. His duties can range from setting a broken leg, to putting a dog to sleep, to treatment for heat exhaustion.

As mentioned before, when you adopt an ex-racer, try to find out exactly why he was retired. If he just wasn't fast enough, that's one thing. But if he was retired due to an injury, it may prevent him from participating in certain activities. This is especially important if you want to adopt a dog to accompany you while jogging or to take lure coursing.

Ajax takes a walk down Memory Lane as he visits his old boarding school—the Seabrook, New Hampshire Race Track. Although he was glad to see Chris Makepeace again, he was equally glad to go home!

A DAY IN A RACING DOG'S LIFE

From this chapter, you now know certain things about how racing dogs live and are trained. To sum up, the following generalizations can be made:

- Racing dogs are used to rising early.

- Racing dogs are used to a strict routine.

- Racing dogs are used to being handled.

- Racing dogs are used to music.

- Racing dogs are used to walking obediently on a lead.

- Racing dogs are used to being around other racing dogs.

- Racing dogs are used to four turnouts daily.

- Racing dogs are used to being around people.

Remember, the more you know about your dog's past, the better equipped you will be to give him the best future possible.

Chapter Four

In a Home

When bringing a retired racer into your home for the first time, the one thing to keep in mind is that everything is completely new to him. I don't just mean that the surroundings are unfamiliar, I mean that being in a house is a new experience. Also new is riding in a car (as opposed to a kennel truck), being around more people than dogs, climbing stairs, looking out windows, adapting to your routine and a myriad of other things that we regard as commonplace.

Racing Greyhounds lead a very insular life. From the time they are born until the day you bring them home, the only life they know is that of the kennel. They might as well be from another planet as far as their knowledge of the "real" world goes. Take heart, though. Greyhounds are not only very intelligent animals, they are also very intuitive. As such, their adjustment period is probably shorter than it would be for other breeds.

SEPARATION ANXIETY

As I said earlier, Greyhounds are dogs that have been bred to get along with other animals. Consequently, they tend to blend in with other pets that you might have. However, if you have no other pets, particularly no other dogs, being alone may be a little scary for your Greyhound. You see, never before have they been without other dogs, and sometimes they are initially overwhelmed by the fact that there is no other canine to reassure them.

52

In most cases, the Greyhound will transfer his desire for companionship to you. In practical terms, what this means is that you can expect the dog to follow you from room to room until he becomes accustomed to his new home and routine. My dog, King, was so intent on keeping me within sight that for the first few months he would even follow me into the bathroom! At the time he was the only dog I had. By the time I adopted my second Greyhound, Ajax, I not only still had King, but I had also adopted a stray Afghan Hound named Jasper.

TWO'S COMPANY

I suspect that the reason Ajax never clung to me as much as King did is that he came into a multi-dog family. Don't get me wrong—Ajax is very affectionate and would always choose to be with me rather than stay home, but he never exhibited a need for my company, merely the desire. If you are having excessive difficulty acclimating your new Greyhound to being left alone, do consider getting another dog, preferably another Greyhound. It may seem inconceivable to you, if you are having trouble with one, that getting another will actually be easier, but, believe me, it often works wonders!

Some cases of so-called separation anxiety are really just a part of your new pet getting settled in to your routine. One of the best things you can do during the first week or so that you have your dog is to take time off from work. That way you can help him adjust to life at your house. Keep in mind that you will get out of the relationship only as much as you put into it. Many people comment on how calm and well-acclimated my dogs are, but I am quick to point out that they didn't necessarily come that way. It takes time, patience and training.

If you are able to take some time off, make sure you spend part of that time away from the dog. While that may sound like a contradiction, it's very important to your dog's acclimatization. I have dubbed the following behavior the School Teacher Syndrome, because every spring I am approached by teachers who want to adopt a Greyhound after the school term is over so that they can spend the entire summer with the dog. I used to think this was a good idea too until I realized that what they were actually doing was putting off the inevitable. When the school term rolled around again, that's when the dogs would have the separation problems and that's when I would get the calls that I would normally expect to get from someone who had a dog for a few days rather than a few months. There is no point in getting the dog used to your being around full-time when, in fact, after a week or after a summer you're going to be back at work. Spend part of each day away so the dog can get used to being alone and to knowing that when you go out, you also come back.

While it is tempting to make a big fuss over your dog when you come home, try to resist. Stay calm and nonchalant. If you gush over the dog and tell him everything is okay, you are reinforcing the idea that everything was not okay while you were gone. The truth is, you need to have a life and you need to be able to leave your house. Your dog needs a life too, so try not to make a big deal of either coming or going.

To make life easier for him while you are gone, try duplicating the "mood music" that the racing kennels use. Some people have found that talk radio is effective, while others claim television works best.

Toys, especially of the stuffed variety, may be comforting to him, as may be an item of your clothing with your scent on it. To keep him busy, get a sterilized, hollowed-out marrow bone and stuff the center with either peanut butter or soft cheese. The idea is that the dog will spend the day trying to get the treat out from the center. You can restuff it every day if he happens to have cleaned it out, but that is unlikely. The filling should be buried deep enough to have a tantalizing scent but be just out of reach

They say a tired dog is a good dog, so before you leave for an extended period try to give your dog a good run or a brisk walk. If that isn't always possible, then play with him at home by tossing toys around the living room or getting him to follow you up and down the steps. It's a great workout for you, too!

If possible, get a friend, relative, neighbor or dog-walking service to take your dog out midday. While a dog can technically "hold it" for many hours, the emotional contact midday is useful

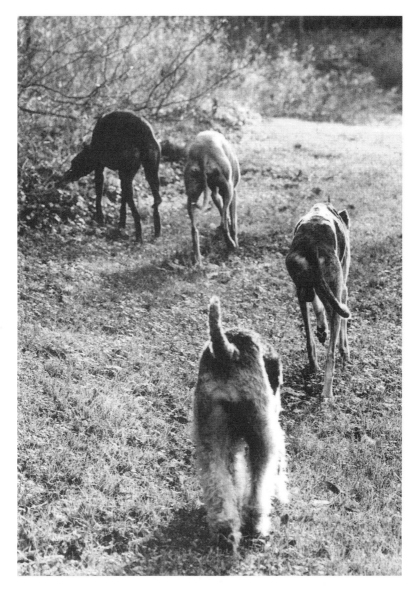

Most Greyhounds are comforted by the presence of other dogs.

and is especially helpful during the critical first few weeks. Whoever you get for that job, make sure he or she understands about never letting the Greyhound off-lead. This includes professional dog walkers as well. They must understand that the ex-racer is not like a Golden Retriever or German Shepherd.

Have you considered the possibility that you may be able to bring your dog to work? In some settings that would be impossible, of course, but in others, who knows? Perhaps there are no dogs where you work because no one ever thought to ask. Also, is there someone in your neighborhood who doesn't work or who works at home? Perhaps that person would enjoy dog sitting for you while you're gone. A Greyhound could be a great companion for a retired person who might not want the commitment of a dog full-time but would love to spend the day with one. Get creative.

Only rarely does a Greyhound have a clinical case of separation anxiety. In this circumstance, the dog cannot be crated or he will hurt himself, but if he is left out, he will destroy the house. The answer is either to find a way that the dog will never be alone (a virtual impossibility) or to take the dog to a veterinary behaviorist who will prescribe a combination of specific desensitization training methods and a low dose of either an anti-anxiety drug or an anti-depressant. I cannot stress enough that this is the method of last resort. Too many people, and, sadly, too many veterinarians, are quick to give a dog a pill if he is not instantly acclimating perfectly. Like people, some dogs just take a little longer than others to adjust to new situations, and some are naturally less outgoing than others. It does not mean something is wrong with them. Remember: Time, patience and training cure most problems. Low doses of drugs can work wonders, but should only be considered after all else has failed. Even then, they should be prescribed only in conjunction with behavioral training and a complete physical examination.

In an ideal world, we could all stay home with our dogs and never have to leave them. In reality, though, most of us work away from home. What does this mean to a dog that is unsure of himself? That all depends on how you approach your absences.

HOW NOT TO BEGIN

Let me give you the worst-case scenario first.

A couple adopts a Greyhound, fresh off the track, on a weekday afternoon. They spend the evening with the dog and half the neighborhood who always wanted to see what a Greyhound looks like up close. The dog is given pizza by a child, whose parents think it's funny. The couple, in all the commotion, forgets to take the dog out, so he lifts his leg against the wall. The dog is hit hard with a newspaper. Because the dog seems so subdued the next morning, the couple decides it's okay to allow him the run of the house when they go to work.

When they get home they find that not only was the dog not housebroken, but that he has eaten their bedspread and clawed the doors to shreds. He has drunk water from the toilet, which contained a cleaning solution that caused him to vomit on the sofa. He has also knocked the dishes from the drain board in the kitchen onto the floor (cutting himself in the process) and has left a trail of blood all over the house. At this point the dog is in a weakened condition and requires immediate veterinary care.

HOW TO AVOID PROBLEMS

Where did the couple go wrong?

The entire problem could have been avoided by the use of a dog crate.

In adopting out retired racers, I cannot stress strongly enough to people how the use of a crate will make their lives easier as well as ease the transition for their new dog. I don't know how many times I've been asked, "But isn't it cruel to keep a dog confined?" My answer is the same every time: "Isn't it more cruel to subject a dog to the many hidden hazards around an unfamiliar house? Isn't it more cruel to return the dog after a few days because you've found him unmanageable?" To paraphrase Robert Frost, "Good crates make good dogs."

HOW TO MAKE A GOOD START

Now here's how the above scenario should have gone.

A couple adopts a Greyhound, fresh off the track, on a weekday afternoon. They spend a quiet evening with the dog, allowing him to get used to them and his new surroundings gradually. Although all of their friends and neighbors are eager to stop by and meet the new addition to the family, the couple decides that the dog has enough to contend with just checking out his new home.

The dog is given a medium-sized dinner and plenty of water, since dogs that have been recently transported are often dehydrated. The dog is taken out often, including within twenty minutes of eating and right before bed. Each time he defecates or urinates outside he is praised. If he does have an accident in the house he is told "No" firmly but without anger or shouting. He is never beaten for an accident.

Knowing that the dog is a little scared by all of the changes, the couple sets up a crate in their bedroom. The dog cries and whimpers initially, but after a half hour or so he quiets down and they all go to sleep.

The couple has arranged to take the next few days off from work—first the wife for two or three days, then the husband. That way the dog can get to know both of them equally and they can show him the ropes. Whenever they have to go out during the day without him, they put him in the crate, which is brought into the kitchen or living room during the day. Fresh water is always available in the crate. As time goes on and they are sure the dog is housebroken and will not destroy the house if left alone, the dog is weaned from the crate gradually.

That is an ideal scenario. Sometimes, however, the ideal is impossible. What if, for example, the couple was unable to take time off from work? In that case, perhaps someone can look in on the dog during a lunch break. Or what if someone in the family was sick when the dog arrived? Maybe a friend or neighbor can help out. If that isn't possible, you can advertise for (or ask your vet to recommend) a dog walker. Retired people often welcome the extra money and are glad for something to do. Also, music or a talk show left playing on the radio is often soothing to the new dog. Just do the best you can, introduce things gradually to your dog and, above all, have patience.

Again, in the case of my Ajax, I used the following method of allowing him free rein in the house while he was getting acclimated. The first four nights he slept in the crate. By the way, on the first night, as soon as I opened the door to the crate he practically ran in. The second night he walked in. The third night he walked in very slowly, and on the fourth night he needed a small push. By the fifth night I had observed him enough to know that he could be trusted to neither chase the cats nor fight with the other dogs. I told him he could sleep uncrated on a trial basis. He was perfect and has not spent a night in a crate since.

The first night will undoubtedly be the hardest. Many dogs cry with anxiety. Don't worry; eventually they stop. Having the crate in your bedroom helps. Bear in mind that it is only natural that a dog will express to you that he is feeling lonely or scared. Be kind, have compassion and put yourself in his position. Wouldn't you be upset if the situation were reversed and suddenly you were forced to live in a kennel surrounded by dogs and no people?

If you have trouble getting your Greyhound to go in the crate, you're not alone. I must have had hundreds of calls from people who have told me they were having the same trouble. I find it somewhat amusing to hear how quickly the dogs can size up someone with a weak will. Ex-racers have spent their entire lives in a crate, and while I can understand that they are eager to get a taste of freedom, they are fully capable of going in if they know you mean it. I am not suggesting that we duplicate their regimented existence at the track, but you need to remember that the crate is not a punishment. It is a useful training tool and a safe haven for your dog.

The real issue here is a matter of will: they do not want to go in the crate, and you want them to. So, who is in charge, you or the dog? It is unwise to let them make the decision on the crate issue for two reasons. First, it teaches them that they are in charge, not you. That is not the message you want to give.

Second, you are crating them as much for their own good as for the sake of your house. An unhousebroken, nervous Greyhound could get hurt in your house if left alone too soon. The crate can protect him.

The following method of getting your dog in the crate is pretty foolproof. Lead him to the crate. Tell him to "kennel up" (a common phrase at the track). If he won't, snap your fingers and repeat the phrase using a firm voice. Do not shout, mind you, but do use a voice that means business. If he still won't, try a little shove. If he won't still, toss in a piece of something delectable such as a small piece of ham or liverwurst. If he won't after that, I suspect you have not mastered the tone of authority. Try again, and imagine you are a busy trainer at a track. Believe me, the dogs go in their crates at the track and they will go in for you too!

CRATES

There are two basic types of crates: hard-molded plastic (the kind used for transporting dogs by air) and wire (often collapsible). Either type is acceptable but I much prefer the plastic type, for the following reasons. Plastic crates are less expensive, sometimes half the price of a wire crate. A plastic crate in a size suitable for a Greyhound can be bought for well under a hundred dollars from discount pet supply stores or catalogs. They are also more denlike, which is the atmosphere a crate is duplicating. But the biggest advantage is that they make escapes very rare. Whenever people call to tell me that their dog has broken out of a crate, I can practically put money on it that they use a wire crate. Plastic crates were designed for airline travel, and you can be sure that airlines do not want dogs running loose in the belly of the plane!

I have heard of two complaints about plastic crates that deserve discussion. Some say that plastic crates do not offer adequate ventilation. This is untrue, as they have a full wire door as well as ventilation slats on both sides. If a dog was left in the direct sun in a plastic crate, it would probably get uncomfortable. That would be true of a wire crate too, but with the

Maddie enjoys getting away from it all in her crate.

added disadvantage of no shade. (There are, by the way, battery-operated clip-on fans with rubber blades. These fans can be attached to the door of a crate and offer relief in extreme heat.) The other complaint about plastic crates is that they are big, bulky and, let's face it, not too attractive. Yes, although they are designed with top and bottom halves that are detachable (which makes storage easy) they are guilty of, shall we say, not adding to home decor. Just keep in mind how useful they are and you will soon view your big, ugly crate as your dog's (and your) best friend.

To give wire crates their due, they do have two advantages over plastic ones. Wire crates provide better visibility. This can sometimes be a comfort to an anxious dog. The other advantage is that they are collapsible, which can come in handy when you are traveling with your pet.

Most Greyhounds need a crate of the following dimensions: 27 inches wide by 40 inches deep by 30 inches high. This is often known as a 500-size crate. Some of the very large males may need the next larger size (a 700) with the following dimensions: 32 inches wide by 48 inches deep by 35 inches high. If you get one much bigger than is actually needed, you will increase the chances of the dog soiling his crate because he will have enough room to move away from the mess.

WEANING FROM THE CRATE

All of the above must be combined with the rarest of commodities—common sense. If, when you feel the dog is trustworthy, you decide to leave him alone uncrated, you must make sure that the house is relatively dog-proof. Don't leave anything of value or anything that could potentially harm your dog within his reach. Scan each room in your house before you leave. If there is an irreplaceable photo of Great-Aunt Bertha on the coffee table, move it. Is that a can of caustic drain opener beneath the sink? Move it. Use your imagination as to what might interest your dog. You can be sure he will!

The weaning from the crate is a gradual process. Don't expect to leave your dog alone for eight hours on the first try. My experience with Ajax illustrates one way of approaching this. Since I work at home, it was a relatively easy process. He would be uncrated during the day except when I had to go out. After four

Sophie in a wire crate that is too small.

or five days I began leaving him uncrated for very short periods, such as the ten minutes it would take me to get a quart of milk at the corner store. The next day I would try him uncrated for twenty minutes while I ran a few errands. Within about ten days I felt comfortable enough to leave him uncrated for several hours. So far, seven years later, he has never betrayed my trust.

OTHER CHALLENGES

Four things that may be obstacles to your new Greyhound are smooth or highly waxed floors (such as in the kitchen), windows, swimming pools and stairs. If you approach each obstacle with patience and understanding, it won't be an obstacle for long.

Smooth Floors

Most Greyhounds never walk on really smooth floors during their racing days. The surfaces in and around the kennel and track are mostly dirt, clay or sand. Some Greyhounds walk on smooth floors without a hitch. For others, however, it appears to be a terrifying ordeal.

My own kitchen floor is linoleum, although not terribly smooth and certainly not very shiny. Neither of my Greyhounds has any trouble with it. However, when I take Ajax with me to give speeches about Greyhound adoption to service organizations and clubs, the meetings are often held in municipal buildings with very smooth, highly polished floors. The first time we went out in tandem, I'm afraid he didn't come off as a very good "AmbassaDog®." As we entered the hall it was as if Ajax was walking on ice. All four legs splayed out, and he had a lot of difficulty just standing upright, much less walking. With much coaxing, and with the use of a blanket on the floor, I was able to inch him across the room to the podium. Now he has the hang of it and could probably race around the room if given half a chance.

If your dog has trouble on smooth floors at home, get pieces of scrap carpeting that he can walk on. Scatter the patches on the floor so that there are small carpet-free areas that he must use. Gradually, over the course of the next few days, remove the pieces of carpet one by one, and you probably won't need them again. There is also a resin-based product on the market that you can spray on your dog's pads to help him get a better grip. I doubt it will ever become necessary to use, but if your dog is having an especially hard time, this product is available at pet supply stores and is made just for dogs' paws, so it is safe.

This may be a good time to check the length of your dog's toenails. Usually they are kept fairly short for racing, but it's possible that they have grown too long. It is very difficult for a dog to walk properly if his toenails are untrimmed. It throws the weight of the foot toward the heel and allows him less maneuverability. Unless you are an expert, I recommend taking him to your local grooming parlor for a trimming. An appointment is often unnecessary, it only costs a few dollars and your dog will feel better and walk better. Once you learn how to do it, a biweekly trimming will keep them in fine shape. You can also ask your veterinarian to trim your dog's nails during an office visit. Most will do it gratis. Cutting extremely long nails can require general

The correct way to trim toenails.

anesthesia since it can be a painful procedure. Please, don't ever let them get that long.

WINDOWS

At the racetrack, and in a kennel environment, racing Greyhounds have limited opportunity to actually look out a window. I'm not suggesting that they are kept in the dark, but they are generally either outside exercising or in the kennel building. Once inside, they mostly have a view from their crate onto an aisle facing other dogs. In the kennel trucks in which they are transported there are no windows, only louvers that can be opened for ventilation.

Because of this, windows are a new experience for your dog, and many are delighted with their expanded view of the world. It's hard to imagine how windows could pose a threat, but they can. Here are two examples of the many I've heard.

Before I adopted King he had been in several other adoptive homes. In the first home he had a near-fatal accident involving a window. He had only lived there two days when he was running around the house playing with the other dogs. In his excitement,

King ran right through a sliding glass door because he didn't recognize it as something solid. He managed to sever an artery in his leg, and his owners got him to the vet just in time to save his life. He bears the scar to this day.

In another incident, a retired racer in North Carolina by the name of Logan leapt through a bedroom window in pursuit of a squirrel that was outside. She, too, was unaware of the fact that windows are solid. Fortunately she was unharmed, and I think her owner was more shaken by it than she was.

The point here is that it's a good idea to introduce your dog to any windows that he has even a remote chance of leaping through. The simplest way to teach him is simply to lead him over to the window and knock on it. You may also want to put his nose or paw against it so he can actually feel that it is solid. Some people put stickers or opaque tape on their windows, but I have found that the knocking/touching method works quite well. By the way, don't forget car windows!

SWIMMING POOLS

In-ground swimming pools are very common in some parts of the country. Naturally, Greyhounds are unfamiliar with them and, as with windows, they need a guided tour in order to avoid a potentially fatal mishap. Like all dogs, Greyhounds can swim, but the water level must be high enough so that they can climb out. A dog that is frightened may not be able to tread water for very long.

If you allow your Greyhound to run in a yard next to an in-ground pool, walk the dog over to the pool and make sure he understands that it contains water and is not a solid surface. This also applies to in-ground, indoor pools. One of our foster homes has an indoor lap pool, and a drenched Greyhound was very surprised when he discovered he couldn't walk on water! Fortunately his temporary owners were there to help him out.

Covered pools are no less of a hazard. People who are good swimmers have been known to drown in covered pools if they fall through; disorientation seems to set in almost immediately.

The same applies to dogs, so make sure they understand that the cover is, at best, a flimsy surface and that water is underneath.

The best solution is to erect a fence around the pool and to keep that area off-limits to your dogs.

STAIRS

And now, for a match not made in heaven: Greyhounds and stairs. This is a tricky subject because dogs adapt to stairs in various ways. One thing is for certain, almost all of them exhibit some degree of trepidation. I believe there are two reasons for this. One is that stair-climbing is something new. The second reason has to do with their anatomy. Greyhounds are, quite obviously, very tall dogs. When you combine that with the highly developed muscles in their legs, you have an animal that bends somewhat differently from other dogs. He is built for flat-out racing, and the bulky leg muscles are something of a hindrance when it comes to steep inclines or declines. Also, the relatively short risers and narrow treads of most stairs make it very difficult for long-legged dogs.

Here's what you can do to make it easier for your dog. First of all, as was suggested for smooth floors, make the surface of your stairs as slip-free as possible. Get rubber or carpeted stair treads. Also, keep the stairs well lit, because it's always easier to accomplish anything when you can see what you're doing.

If the stairs have open backs (risers), it is helpful to the dog if you enclose them, either with wood or with clear acrylic if you want to preserve the open look. I know of one dog whose leg slipped and was broken in open-backed stairs. It was painful for the dog as well as traumatic to both the dog and her owner.

Be gentle and patient with your dog. You may find his fear of stairs silly, but it's very serious to him. Whatever you do, don't force him. You may wind up traumatizing him and turning what could have been a simple training job into a major production.

It's ideal if there are two people available to coax him up the steps—preferably close to the wall for security. One person can gently tug on the leash while the other can gently push from behind. If you have to go it alone, assume the rear position. It's futile to attempt to pull the dog up the steps by his leash. It reminds me a lot of the days when I was adopting out wild burros rescued from the Grand Canyon and Death Valley by The Fund for Animals. Before we learned the right way to do it, we would often attempt to pull the burros into the van. Needless to say, we failed. The burro would simply sit down, and that was the end of it. It wasn't until we learned to wrap the lead rope behind the hind legs and inch him forward that we made any progress. I applied this principle to Greyhounds and, presto, it worked! Put one of your arms behind the dog's rear legs, just above the hock,

Alexandra is helped up the stairs.

and nudge him forward. To descend, repeat the process, taking great care not to push him down the steps.

Quite often the Greyhound will take the steps three or more at a time. That's okay—at least he's moving forward! Eventually he will learn that he can relax going up and down steps and will take them one at a time.

If you have narrow, winding or steep steps (I have all three) it's going to take longer for the dog to get acclimated. Again, just be patient. Once the dog realizes that he's missing out on some good times by not climbing steps, he'll make an extra effort. As always, when he is successful give him lots of praise.

GREYHOUNDS AND CHILDREN

Many people who adopt a Greyhound do so because the breed has a reputation for being good with children. Generally speaking, this is true. However, there are a few things about ex-racers and children that bear mentioning, as well as several rules of safety that parents must teach their children to follow with any breed of dog. Greyhounds are, on the whole, a gentle breed, but any dog that is a stranger to you and your family should be approached with caution.

One thing to remember about ex-racers is that although they are docile dogs, they have not had a great deal of experience with children. Whether you are choosing your own dog or one is being chosen for you, make sure the Greyhound you bring home is easy-going and friendly. A very shy or retiring dog is likely to be upset by the noise and erratic movements of children. Likewise, a dog that is too outgoing and active may knock over very small children or want to try to dominate them. What you want is a dog that will be thrilled by the sight of children and want to play with them. You want a calm dog, but not one that is so calm that he will be frightened or annoyed by loud noises. You also want an active dog but not one that sees playtime as a way to assert his superiority. It's a fine line, but the adoption group should be able to help you.

Once you get your dog home, keep in mind that everything is new to him. Allow him to ease into his new environment with as little pressure as possible. In other words, the demands on him should be few—even the demand that he be affectionate or playful. He has a lot to absorb, so take it easy on him and let him make the first move toward you and your children. In the beginning, your new Greyhound needs a lot of time out. Even a well-intentioned hug can be too much.

To the extent that your children are capable of understanding, try to impress on them that although they are excited to have a new dog in the house and have had a lot of time to prepare for him, the new dog was just thrust into the situation. Because of that the dog is going to need time to feel like he's a member of the family. Reading to your children Chapter Three, "The Racing Life," which describes what the Greyhound's life was like on the track, should help them appreciate how strange living in a house must be to your dog.

LET SLEEPING DOGS LIE

One fact about track life that is especially pertinent to a Greyhound's new life as a companion is that at the track Greyhounds slept in crates. Because of that they were never touched or disturbed in any way while they were asleep. To do so now might startle and frighten them, and it is possible that they could wake up and snap at the source of the disturbance. This is not due to any inherent viciousness, but, rather, it is more of a conditioned reflex. Both you and your children should learn to awaken the dog before touching him. Some Greyhounds have an odd habit of sleeping with their eyes half open. To the untutored eye it can look as if they are awake. The only way to tell the difference is to call the dog's name and see that he has responded and is really focusing on you. At that point, feel free to pet him, but even then, hugging him or standing over his bed in a way that seems threatening to him may be too much in the beginning.

CRATE ETIQUETTE

Another thing about track life that has bearing on a Greyhound's new life in a home is that in his previous life he had very few things of his own. The crate was one of them, and for this reason, some Greyhounds feel possessive of it. No child should ever go into a crate with any dog. It is not cute or charming, and it has the potential to end badly. Any dog, and especially one whose sole possession in life has been his crate, might feel either territorial or threatened in the confined space. *Never* allow a child to go into a crate, whether the dog is in it or not.

A dog bed can, in some cases, translate into a crate in the minds of some dogs. Which is why leaning over a dog while he is on his bed, or hugging him, can be perceived as a threat. Certainly in the beginning it is best to restrict your affection to the dog to times when he is standing up, fully awake and in a receptive mood. You can read his body language to tell how he is feeling. If his tail is up and wagging, if he is smiling (not to be confused with the baring of teeth) or if he makes a move toward you with an open and pleasant expression on his face, then he is friendly and ready for a pat on the head or shoulder. Do not let your child hug a new Greyhound or any other strange dog. This is commonly interpreted by dogs as dominant and threatening behavior.

DON'T LEAVE KIDS ALONE WITH DOGS

Children must always be supervised when interacting with the new dog. Do not allow them to be alone together—not even for "just a minute." In the few instances when I've received calls from people who have told me a Greyhound has snapped at their child, I always ask the same question: What was the child doing at the time? Often the answer has been that they didn't know—they weren't in the room. Children can provoke dogs, either accidentally or on purpose, just to see what the reaction will be. It is up to the parents or a responsible adult to supervise children's interaction with dogs. Keep children away from the dog's face, do not allow the dog to be hugged by them, do not allow them to taunt the dog (either physically or verbally) and, when you see that the dog is feeling tired or expressing in some way that he wants to be left alone, call for a time-out. Put the dog in his crate or have the children go into another room for awhile.

BE CAREFUL AFTER SURGERY OR AN INJURY

After being spayed or neutered, Greyhounds, like anyone who has just had major surgery, are especially tender and sensitive. Be sure they are given ample quiet time, that they are not handled excessively and that they are not allowed (or encouraged) to engage in boisterous play.

Some Greyhounds that were retired because of a leg injury, either a healing broken leg or a torn or pulled ligament or tendon, can still be sore. Make sure that your children know where the pain is and that they avoid the area. They must be careful neither to touch it nor to lean on it. A dog that is experiencing a sudden sharp pain might well snap at the source of the pain.

FOOD TIME IS PRIVATE TIME

Children must never be allowed to play near a dog's food bowl while the dog is eating. Likewise, children must never try to remove a piece of rawhide or a toy from a dog's mouth. I strongly discourage feeding bits of your food from the table while you are eating. It turns the dog into a beggar, and, if you have more than one dog, there can be a fight over which one gets the morsel. Your child's fingers or face could be caught in the middle.

KEEP DOORS AND FENCE GATES CLOSED

It must be impressed on children that Greyhounds can never be allowed to run loose in an unfenced area. Ideally the outside area around the door that is most often used in your house will already be fenced. This is something that most adoption groups require. But if this is not the case in your home, then you must teach your children never to stand in a doorway with the door open. Maintain a policy of "Go in or go out, but close the door behind you." To prevent accidents, put up a gate in a hallway near a door to prevent the dog from darting out of an open door. It can also serve as a reminder to the children that Greyhounds cannot go out unleashed.

Remind children, too, to close outside fence gates as they enter or exit. A spring attached to the gate to pull it shut is a good back-up plan. Toddlers who are too young to understand the seriousness of the situation can sometimes open a front door before you even know what's happening. A hook-and-eye latch will prevent such an accident. Another potential hazard exists in houses where an inside house door leads to the garage. If both the garage door and the house door are left open, the dog can escape that way. Again, be mindful of the potential for tragedy, stay alert and keep those doors and gates closed.

GREYHOUNDS AND KIDS CAN BE GREAT TOGETHER

Despite all of the above warnings, most Greyhounds and kids live together happily. When you are a child, nothing compares to

Alice and Ike are best buddies.

having a dog as your very best friend. As adults, some of our fondest memories of growing up are of good times with the family dog. I am merely trying to prevent accidents from happening. That way you, your children and your new Greyhound can live happily ever after!

CREATING A SECURE ENVIRONMENT

The final piece of advice I have for acclimating your new addition to the family is to give him a special place of his own. He will have his crate, of course, and some people choose to make it available by leaving the door open long after the dog actually "needs" it. But eventually you will want him to get more into the swing of things. What often does the trick is his own soft dog bed or a plump comforter. He will soon recognize it as his own spot and become quite attached to it. From that vantage point he can watch his new family and figure out just where he's going to fit in.

CHOOSING THE BEST VETERINARIAN

There are a few other things you should do in advance of the dog's arrival. First of all, if you don't already have a veterinarian, now is a good time to interview some. Just because you have located a vet near you, or if you already have someone you have been using for years, does not mean he or she is the best choice for your new Greyhound. What you need is not just a good vet but a vet who is aware of the special nature and idiosyncrasies of Greyhounds.

Call and ask if the veterinarian has other Greyhounds as clients. If not, what about other sighthounds (Afghans, Borzois and so on)? As you will learn in later chapters, sighthounds really are different, and you don't want to use a vet who is treating one for the first time. If possible, get the adoption center to recommend a good, qualified veterinarian in your area. Even if you have to drive a little farther, it's worth it to get a suitable doctor.

In addition to technical expertise, try to find a vet with whom you have a good rapport. He or she should be willing to answer

King relaxing in his bed.

all of your questions, take your concerns seriously and anticipate your dog's needs. If you question what experience he or she has had with Greyhounds, the vet should welcome it as a sign of your commitment to your dog rather than as an attack on his or her professionalism. Remember, you will be putting your dog's life in this person's hands.

I also recommend that you do some comparison shopping as to the vet's rates. One man who adopted a Greyhound from me recently was charged double what my vet charges just for a basic office visit! All tests and shots were extra, of course. Look for a veterinarian who is knowledgeable about sighthounds, has a humane outlook and offers good rates.

Even if your Greyhound comes to you spayed or neutered and fully inoculated, I suggest taking him to your veterinarian for a checkup. Most adoption kennels are overworked, and it is possible that yours did not have the time or the staff to give your dog a complete examination. Besides, it's a good idea for your vet to see your dog at least once when he is well, so that if he becomes ill, there will be a point of comparison.

Have your dog weighed, and get a routine examination of eyes, ears, heart, lungs and teeth. Have your dog tested for heartworm and the presence of the four most prevalent tick-borne diseases (Lyme, Rocky Mountain Spotted Fever, Ehrliciosis and Babesiosis) if this has not already been done. For a complete discussion of tick-borne diseases, please see Chapter Five, "Care and Feeding." If a fecal test has not been done recently, bring in a fresh stool sample.

If you have other pets, you would be wise to isolate your new Greyhound from them unless he has had all of his shots as well as a negative fecal test. The chance that he has an infectious disease is slim, but why risk it at all? Many racing kennels do not inoculate their dogs after the first year on the theory that since they are associating only with each other, they cannot pick up any illnesses. This, of course, is shortsighted. Some diseases, such as parvovirus, are airborne. Others, such as rabies, could be transmitted if a rabid raccoon somehow wandered into a kennel's turnout pen and bit a dog. On the East Coast in 1991 there was a virtual rabies epidemic, so it is essential that these dogs be protected immediately.

GET YOUR SUPPLIES IN ADVANCE

Finally, before your dog arrives, get a supply of food, feeding and water bowls, a collar and leash (if they are not provided), a crate and a soft bed. You can also purchase an identification tag for your new dog in advance. It doesn't matter if you don't know yet what you are going to name him. The important information on the tag is your name, address and phone number. If the worst happened and your new dog was lost within a few days of his arrival, he would be in double trouble. He would not only be unfamiliar with you and your neighborhood, he would also be unfamiliar with life outside the track. Even if the adoption group puts one of their tags on your dog, you need one with your own vital statistics. That way if your dog runs off and winds up at a house around the corner, the people can contact you directly and the return will be made that much easier and quicker.

Once you have all of your supplies, you can bring your dog into his new environment and spend your time getting to know him rather than dashing out to go shopping. There's no sense letting anything interfere with the wonderful adventure you two are about to embark on together.

Chapter Five

Care and Feeding

*I*n Chapter Three, we discussed the importance of a good diet for a racing dog. However, since your dog is no longer a professional athlete, what should he be fed now? First, let's examine exactly what racing dogs are fed at the track. The idea here, of course, is not to duplicate it but, rather, to diverge gradually from that regimen. If you change your dog's diet too quickly, he is likely to experience anything from mild gastric disturbances (such as gas) to diarrhea.

THE TRACK DIET

The emphasis at the racetrack is on performance, and in order to foster it, racing Greyhounds are fed a high-protein, high-carbohydrate diet. Protein, of course, is good for muscle development, and carbohydrates provide energy for the long haul.

Compared to other breeds of dog, Greyhounds at the track are fed enormous quantities of food. Because they burn off so many calories during a race, it would be easy for them to lose a lot of weight. The trainers compensate by feeding them more than most dogs their size eat. Typically, the males are fed 2$^1/_2$ pounds a day, and the females, 2 pounds.

Each kennel has its own recipe, but the basics always include raw beef mixed with a high-protein dry food. Added to that can be vegetables (often spinach or turnip greens for extra iron), corn oil (for the coat), salt (to replace what is lost during a race), water (to compensate for the extra salt), powdered vitamins and electrolytes. Bowls of water are kept filled in each crate.

INTRODUCING NEW FOOD

The first item you can omit from your dog's new diet is raw meat. Not only can it be rather unpleasant to deal with, but also he doesn't need it. Raw meat can also be the source of food poisoning, including the potentially deadly e-coli bacteria.

If you want him to have meat, substitute a good, high-quality canned dog food that doesn't contain meat by-products. If you knew what those by-products really were, you'd never feed them to your dog. Incidentally, dogs can get by quite well on dry dog food alone. It is, after all, nutritionally balanced. However, I recommend making additions to it in part for variety and in part for added nutrition. Greyhounds just off of the track have never been given dry kibble alone, so don't be surprised if in the beginning they don't really know what to do with it. Many seem to view it as a bowl of cereal without the milk!

If you are only feeding dry food, start with 4 cups per day for the females and 5 cups per day for the males (half in the morning, half in the evening), see how your dog's weight responds and adjust accordingly. Feeding your dog twice a day is important because although he can survive on a once-a-day feeding plan, it puts a much greater burden on his digestive tract. Once-a-day feedings were developed for the convenience of people, but it does not do your dog much of a favor. Dogs fed once a day also are more likely to beg and may become tense or irritable due to low blood sugar.

Since your dog is no longer racing, you should downgrade from a high-protein dry dog food to one that is designed for normal adult maintenance. When your dog reaches the age of seven, you might want to consider a lower-fat or lower-protein food formulated for the "mature" dog.

YOU GET WHAT YOU PAY FOR

Whatever your dog's age, you should go for a high-quality food for a number of reasons. One, the quality brands are often concentrated, which means you don't have to feed as much. Two, they aren't loaded with fillers or the dreaded "meat by-products."

Three, good dry dog food tends to harden the stool, making your clean-up job a lot easier. Four, it is also better for teeth than soft foods or meat alone. And, finally, you will be giving your dog the best ingredients, which, in turn, will keep your dog healthier.

I never recommend giving your dog the individually wrapped burger-type semimoist foods. Not only are they filled with salt, sugar and artificial coloring, but they offer little more than empty calories. They will promote bad teeth, indigestion, and obesity.

As for which brand to use, I recommend trying several kinds and seeing how your dog fares. I started off using one well-known premium brand until I discovered that it was giving several of my dogs gas. I switched brands, and the gas never came back. Yet, other people I know use that particular brand, and their dogs are just fine. The point is, each dog's metabolism is different, just as every person's is. Despite some people's almost fanatical allegiance to one brand of dog food, in truth, there is no one food that is perfect for every dog. Experiment to see which yours likes and which agrees with him. Be careful, however, not to switch foods abruptly. Blend in the old brand with the new gradually over the course of a week. Abrupt changes can cause diarrhea.

CONTINUE WITH VEGETABLES

I am very much in favor of continuing the track's practice of giving Greyhounds vegetables. Dogs are omnivores, not carnivores. What this means is that in the wild, dogs do not eat only meat (as do cats). Dogs eat grasses and other greens, and I believe we do them a great disservice by limiting their diet to meat.

If cooking vegetables is too much for you, try the canned varieties. My dogs are fond of all vegetables, but especially carrots, spinach, stewed tomatoes and cauliflower. Avoid potatoes (unless they are mashed) as well as corn, since most dogs have trouble digesting them.

Scraps from your plate are also good, not as a substitute for a balanced canine diet, but as a supplement. Cooked rice (white or brown) is also a nice addition to his diet and can be helpful in firming up loose stools.

COOKING FOR YOUR DOG

There are three reasons why I cook for my dogs: I enjoy it, I believe it gives them added vitamins and other nutrients and I know it adds variety to their life. I am not suggesting that you substitute a homemade diet for commercially prepared dry food. However, I am suggesting this as an addition to dry food, which should form the basis of their diet.

To cut down on preparation time, I cook for my dogs twice a week and simply dole out refrigerated portions (reheated, of course). I change vegetables often and always combine at least two, such as carrots and spinach. I also cook up a big batch of rice or noodles, and to that I add either well-drained, cooked ground beef or boiled chicken. The mixture can get a little dry, so I add either beef or chicken broth. The consistency should not be that of soup, but more of a stew. At feeding time, twice a day, I give them a cup or so of the stew well mixed with their dry food. The males, which are larger, get 2 cups of dry food, while the females get 1 1/2 cups. As an added treat, every now and then I add a heaping tablespoon of low-fat cottage cheese or a small piece of cheese on top as a garnish and to provide a little extra calcium. To say that they love it is an understatement.

There are a few staples that you can have on hand to add to your dog's food that do not require a lot of work. I am rarely without a container of cottage cheese, a can of mixed vegetable juice, a jar of wheat germ, various cans of vegetables and, of course, some sort of cooked grain (rice, barley, millet and so on). Incidentally, if you plan to feed dry food only, the mixed vegetable juice does wonders for it as does a light sprinkle of grated cheese.

PROS AND CONS OF OIL

I would add oil to a dog's food only if his coat looked dry. Otherwise you are simply adding empty calories to your dog's food, and all that extra fat is no better for your dog than it is for you. Also, if your dog has a tendency toward loose stools, as may well be the case in the beginning, omit the oil, as it will only aggravate the condition. If you ever need to add oil for a dry coat, the best kind to get is one high in essential fatty acids. These are generally found in fish oils (cod liver oil, for example) and provide the most complete nutrition and absorption. A few teaspoons a day will do until the coat is back in shape. A lot of all-purpose oil that people add to their dog's food simply passes through the animal's system without doing any real good.

VITAMIN SUPPLEMENTS

Once the dog is finished racing, electrolytes can be omitted from his diet. Vitamins, however, are a different story. If you take vitamins yourself, you may want to give them to your dog, too. But if the food your dog is getting says "nutritionally complete" on the label (and it should), then extra vitamins may be unnecessary. On the other hand, if you are anything like me, you may want to give your dog vitamins just for good measure. It is generally a good idea to give balanced canine multivitamins as opposed to adding specific ones. Such a practice may add too much of a particular nutrient. My current practice involves blending a powder containing trace minerals and vitamins into the dogs' food. I do this because these particular nutrients are hard to get in any diet—human or canine.

HOW MUCH IS ENOUGH?

Many dogs that are just off the track need a little fattening up. Most people love this process, and so do the dogs. Be careful, though, not to give them too much of a good thing. Greyhounds are lean by nature, and overweight ones can develop joint trouble or arthritis from carrying around more pounds than their frame can handle. A good rule of thumb is that you should be able to feel your Greyhound's ribs easily, but you should not be able to see the outline of them.

In the case of convalescing dogs that need to be coaxed into eating, my theory, which is backed up by veterinarians, is that you do whatever it takes to get something into them. I've found that canned cat food is irresistible. Beef tea, a broth made from round steak, is also quite tempting and is helpful if the dog cannot, or will not, eat solid food. Other delicacies include rice pudding and bottled baby food. One of my elderly Afghan Hounds, Seamus, made a comeback from pneumonia with a diet of toasted ham and cheese sandwiches! Hiding his antibiotics in the melted cheese was also a convenient method of getting the pills down his throat. Please understand that this is not meant to be a full-time diet. But when a dog is extremely ill and it is either junk food or no food, go with the junk. Just make sure they don't get spoiled and want it for the rest of their lives!

When you bring your new Greyhound home, don't try switching brands of food every week. Try a particular diet for a few weeks, and see how it goes. Gas or diarrhea at the beginning may just be a reaction to new food, new water, a new schedule and general stress. In fact, just by switching brands too often and too quickly you may create the very problems (gas and/or diarrhea) that you are trying to avoid.

Because Greyhounds are so tall, it is helpful to them if you feed them on an elevated platform. That way they don't have to gulp their food or stretch their necks too far to get at their dish. This is especially important for older dogs as, with age, a dog's trachea is not as flexible as it once was. An older dog is much more likely to choke or gag on his food if he has to reach down for it. Keep dog bowls elevated 12 to 16 inches from the floor, depending on the height of the dog. By the way, stainless steel or ceramic bowls are the best because you can sterilize them and keep them free of bacteria. Stainless steel bowls have the edge because they are lighter weight and if you drop them, they won't break. Plastic bowls cannot tolerate the high heat required to kill off germs.

WATER, WATER EVERYWHERE

Veteran horse trainer George Millar once told me that water was the cheapest medicine. He was right, of course, and no living creature, dogs included, should ever go thirsty. Water flushes the system, keeps the kidneys in good working order and aids in digestion. Keep the water bowl filled, and make sure you scrub it out on a regular basis.

THYROID TESTING

After you have had your Greyhound for a few months, if you find that he has still not grown any hair on the backs of his legs or stomach, or if he seems lethargic or listless, you may want to have his thyroid function tested. Before I go any further I want to state that a certain amount of misinformation about Greyhounds and hypothyroidism (underactive thyroid) has been circulating to such an extent that some people are giving supplements to dogs that may not need them, thus possibly endangering their dogs in the process. Let me explain.

The endocrine system, of which the thyroid is a part, is complex and not wholly understood. The thyroid gland controls the body's metabolism and secretes either more or less hormones into the bloodstream depending on energy demands. If a dog (or person) is diagnosed a hypothyroid it means that the thyroid is not secreting the appropriate amount of hormones the body needs.

Many factors influence the thyroid level in the body, and a simple T4 test, which is what some veterinarians recommend, is not enough to tell if a dog really is hypothyroid. Thyroid levels are affected by stress, medication and even other diseases. On top of that, some of the tests themselves have certain limitations. For that reason, the only valid diagnosis of hypothyroidism involves both a T3 and T4 check plus a TSH response test (thyroid releasing hormone).

A further complicating factor is that many members of the sighthound family, Greyhounds included, have thyroid levels that are considered borderline low for other breeds. If you give these dogs thyroid supplements, you will be crippling the thyroid function that they have by allowing the gland to, in effect, turn itself off.

To sum up, the only dogs that should receive thyroid supplements are those with test results that are clearly subnormal. Hairless thighs and/or shyness are not necessarily indicative of hypothyroidism; in fact, frequently they are not. Greyhounds should be tested under conditions that are as stress-free as possible (for example, after they have been in a home for a few months), and a complete thyroid panel should be run: T3, T4 and TSH.

TICK-BORNE DISEASES

One of the sad facts of life for Greyhounds in racing kennels is that they do not always receive the best care. One manifestation of this is ticks, the not-so-harmless pests that can transmit deadly diseases.

No national records are being kept on Greyhounds and ticks, but according to Dr. Cynthia Holland, a microbiologist and director of the ProtaTek Reference Laboratory in Chandler, Arizona, since 1995 approximately 40 percent of the Greyhounds she has tested—well over a thousand dogs—are asymptomatic carriers of one or more tick-borne disease agents.

More times than I care to remember, we have received ex-racers just off the track that had literally hundreds of ticks attached to their bodies. It takes several volunteers with tweezers an hour to get them clean. The problem is that although the ticks are removed, the damage that they may have inflicted could be just beginning.

While the symptoms of some tick-borne diseases show up almost immediately, others may lie dormant for years. By then, a dog's owner may well have forgotten that the dog was tick-infested at one time. And, of course, once the disease has reached the chronic phase, it is not only more difficult to treat but more costly as well.

Another problem with tick-borne diseases is that the symptoms can mimic other diseases, which is why they are known as The Great Impostors. For example, lethargy, lameness, seizures, a low platelet count or kidney failure could all be the signs of something other than a tick-borne disease. It is helpful to have a veterinarian who is willing to consider ticks as the culprit.

Yet another aspect of the Greyhound and tick problem is that because Greyhounds travel from track to track, it is highly possible for them to have picked up a tick in one location and taken it with them to an area where such a tick is not native. It is not uncommon, for example, for a Greyhound to be born in Kansas, trained in Arizona, raced in Florida and to wind up in Connecticut. From there he could be adopted by a family in New Jersey. Not many vets in New Jersey are on the lookout for signs of babesiosis because it is almost unheard of in the state. Likewise, most vets in California are not alert to the dangers of Lyme disease in a dog. What you need to do is explain to your veterinarian that although your Greyhound may now be living in a particular locale, he could have been anywhere and exposed to any number of ticks.

The most common tick-borne diseases are Lyme disease, Rocky Mountain spotted fever, ehrlichiosis and babesiosis. When you adopt a Greyhound, ask if the dog had ticks. If so, get him tested. Find out, too, if the dog was ever given a Lyme disease vaccine. If so, when your dog is tested, the titer results will be elevated. Make sure you ask your veterinarian for a panel that will test for all four diseases. If you are questioned, explain how the dog has spent much of his life on the road.

Once the results come in, treatment is a little tricky. There are some veterinarians who do not believe in treating a dog until he shows symptoms. Others rely solely on test results, symptoms or not.

If the results are negative, you may want to consider getting a Lyme vaccine for your Greyhound if you live in a region affected by the disease. Some veterinarians recommend it routinely, while others say that it is only partially effective and that some evidence suggests that the vaccine itself can compromise a dog's immune system.

If the result is positive and the decision is to treat, Doxycycline is the drug of choice for Rocky Mountain, Lyme and ehrlichia. The usual dosage is 500 milligrams twice a day for four weeks. Too short a course or too weak a dose may actually do more harm than good, as it can kill off the weaker bacteria and allow the stronger to thrive. Babesia require the use of either the antibiotic Clindamycin or a drug called imidocarb diproprionate. The latter is not yet approved by the FDA, and its use necessitates a special license which not many veterinarians have. Although it is the most effective weapon against babesia, it can also produce severe side effects. A new form of imidocarb diproprionate called IMI-ZOL® is also an alternative for treating babesia. It is in a sterile solution and is given in two doses, two weeks apart.

Yet another variable involves dogs whose results are borderline. To treat or not to treat? Some vets do; some don't. Certainly, by treating a dog, you will greatly reduce the chances of damage. On the other hand, overuse and misuse of antibiotics, both in humans and in animals, has caused some strains of bacteria to become resistant. If your dog is borderline but not showing symptoms, one course of action might be to wait for six months and retest. If the titer is the same, it probably means that the dog was exposed at some point in his life but that he has fought off the infection.

Combine your intuition with the experience of your veterinarian. A second opinion may be in order.

While all of the above may sound rather grim, bear in mind that except for the most advanced cases, tick-borne diseases are treatable. The key is to test your dog to determine if he is infected, to treat him if he is, and to prevent any further infections. In Chapter Six, I will discuss what types of tick preventatives are safe for Greyhounds.

SPAYING AND NEUTERING

Your visit to the vet is a good time to set up an appointment for the dog to be spayed or neutered if it hasn't been done already. It cannot be overemphasized how important this is. With tens of thousands of Greyhounds, and over thirteen million other dogs, dying every year for the want of a home, one would have to be either incredibly naive or thoughtless to even consider bringing another Greyhound litter into the world. Don't forget that 30 percent of the dogs that wind up in shelters are purebred. No matter how beautiful or talented or good-natured your dog is, there are hundreds more just as good, or even better. So don't think that by breeding your dog you will be creating more "perfect" specimens. Other perfect specimens of all kinds already exist, and they are dying by the millions!

As for breeding ex-racers to other breeds of dogs, or to AKC Greyhounds, forget that too. The bottom line with all breeding is that there are already more dogs (and cats) in the world than there are homes for them. Even if you think you will find good homes for all of the puppies you create, what about the puppies' puppies? And their puppies? And what about the homes you have "taken up" because you chose to breed your dog? You can be sure that other deserving dogs already alive will now die because there is no room for them.

And, if you think that your dog will never be bred because you are just too careful, bear in mind that most mixed-breed dogs are the result of accidental matings. The sexual urge is very strong when a female is in heat and a male is on her trail. Dogs have been known to move heaven and earth to get at the object of their affection. It only takes a moment's inattention from you and it could be too late.

HEALTH ADVANTAGES

The health advantages to spaying and neutering are considerable. Male dogs that have not been neutered are prone to testicular cancer in their older years as well as prostate trouble. Uterine cancer and mammary tumors are common in unspayed females, as is pyrometra, an infection of the uterus than can be fatal if not treated promptly. I have been asked why these diseases do not kill dogs in the wild, and the answer is that in some cases they do. However, because wild dogs are sexually and reproductively active, the various organs are kept in good shape. By contrast, a domestic, unneutered male dog that is constantly stimulated by the odor of females in heat, but that never has the chance to breed, can develop chronic inflammations. Likewise, unspayed females that regularly go into heat but are never bred are also prone to problems. It really is more humane, from many standpoints, to spay and neuter, and many adoption groups have this surgery performed on Greyhounds before they enter their new home.

GROOMING

In general, Greyhounds are very clean and do not need a tremendous amount of care. That does not mean, however, that they should only be bathed once a year whether they need it or not. Grooming allows you to spend quality time with your dog, increases the bond between you and gives you the opportunity to head off potential health problems before they become serious.

If your dog comes to you with fleas, a nontoxic flea bath is in order right away. (See Chapter Six for specific recommendations concerning flea prevention.) The presence of fleas almost surely means the dog has tapeworm, so it would be wise to be on the lookout for telltale rice-like segments in his stools. Otherwise, a bath every six to eight weeks helps remove dead hair and keeps him smelling fresh. Always use a shampoo made specifically for dogs. Human shampoo will dry out a dog's skin even with only one washing because the pH balance of dog skin is different from ours.

The Best Way to Bathe Your Dog

Do not bathe your dog in cold water. Even on the hottest summer day, a Greyhound can become deeply chilled by the icy water of a garden hose. It is a very simple matter for a plumber to install hot and cold faucets on your outside water spigot. Then you can attach a U-shaped hose that connects to both faucets and attach that to a regular hose. Just blend the hot with the cold

A plumber can easily install hot and cold running water outside.

until you've reached a comfortable temperature. The cool side of room temperature should be fine.

The ideal way to bathe your dog is in a tub at your waist level. That way you won't strain your back bending over and you'll be able to get a better look at the dog. If that is not possible, your regular tub will do. You may want to have someone hold the dog, or you can simply tie his leash to the water faucets so that he can stand comfortably but cannot escape. Be sure to provide a non-slip surface on the bottom of the tub.

You should get a device for the faucet that acts as a shower or spray. if you don't have one, then fill a plastic bowl (*not* glass, please) with warm water. Plug the dog's ears with cotton, and wet him thoroughly. Next, shampoo, taking care to avoid the eyes and mouth. Rinse thoroughly (shampoo residue can cause flaking skin), repeat as necessary, and you're done. Most Greyhounds will stand quietly for all of this even if they aren't crazy about it! Always dry your dog completely, and, in cold weather, keep him

Some items for grooming (clockwise from bottom left): ear cleaning solution, toenail trimmers, tooth scaler, canine toothbrush and toothpaste and grooming glove.

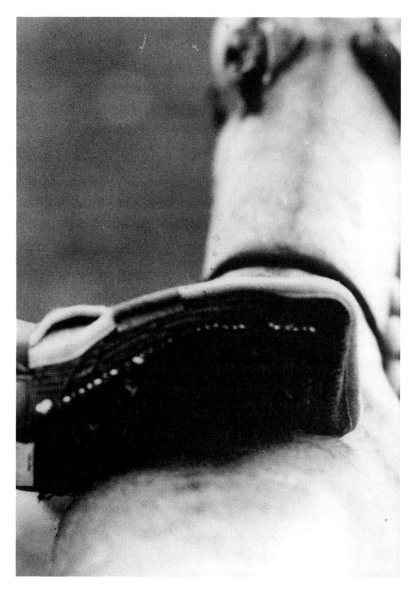

Grooming the coat with the hound glove.

out of drafts and do not allow him outside for several hours after the bath.

While you are bathing him, check his ears for dirt and ticks. If you see dirt, wipe it out with a cotton ball, not a cotton swab. If the dirt has a foul odor or is very thick, he may have an ear infection, so see your veterinarian. Check toenail length at bath time, too.

Finally, brush the coat daily with a flat rubber or sisal glove (called, appropriately enough, a hound glove) or a fine-tooth comb. Most Greyhounds love being brushed and practically purr with delight. You might try a little muscle massage at the same time. You'll soon discover that grooming will become the highlight of the day for both of you.

DENTAL CARE

Most dogs that are just off the track have terrible-looking teeth that are covered with tartar. More than one veterinarian has looked skeptical when told that a certain dog was only two or three when what he or she saw looked more like the mouth of a ten-year-old. The reason is that racing dogs have a totally soft diet, so the tartar builds quickly. Also, many gnaw on their crates out of boredom and wear their teeth down.

Get your dog's teeth cleaned regularly by a veterinarian to prevent tooth loss and gum infection. This can be done initially while the dog is being spayed or neutered so that he has to be anesthetized only once. I cannot stress enough how important it is to keep your dog's teeth clean. Not only is the odor from dirty teeth offensive but, more important, decayed teeth or infected gums can jeopardize your dog's life. Bacteria from mouth infections have a tendency to lodge in the valves of the heart, making them less able to operate properly. A dog can actually die from heart trouble brought on by bad teeth!

To maintain clean teeth, brush your dog's teeth weekly with special dog toothpaste. Your veterinarian will have it available as do pet supply catalogs. Also, hard dog biscuits or sterilized cow hooves help keep dogs' teeth clean, and dogs really love giving them a workout! Many people also give their dogs raw carrots to gnaw on. That way the dogs clean their teeth, massage their gums and get their vitamins all at once!

If you want to get really adventurous, you can try scaling your dog's teeth yourself. Dental tools are available in many pet

Sophie's teeth are scaled to remove tartar.

supply stores. Start at the gum line and gently move the tool back and forth, gradually working your way toward the tip of the tooth. It takes patience, both on the part of the person and the dog, but it can avoid a yearly trip to the veterinarian's office for dentistry. Before you try this, however, you might want to ask your veterinarian to demonstrate the correct technique. If you use too much pressure you could damage the enamel on your dog's teeth.

ASSISTING THE OLDER DOG

A word about the older Greyhound: As with people, a dog's senses become weaker as he ages. Age comes on so gradually that many owners fail to notice that their old friend is not responding the way he used to. Impaired sight or hearing loss puts a dog at a disadvantage. It does not, however, have to mean the end.

I have had the pleasure of sharing my life with many older dogs, and, in fact, several of my dogs were over ten when I adopted them. I sometimes joke that a dog doesn't start to get good until he's at least five! The point is that older dogs have a lot to give, and whatever small sacrifices we have to make to accommodate their needs are well worth it.

Eyesight and Hearing

With age, a dog's eyesight can be diminished either by cataracts or by rods that were damaged earlier in life. Such dogs compensate by relying more and more on their sense of smell. Try to keep your furniture in the same place and always leave a night-light on for them. Keep in mind that very bright sunlight can also be troublesome for older dogs with poor eyesight.

If your dog's hearing should start to fail, have patience, keep him out of harm's way by alerting him to dangers that he may not be able to hear coming and use a gentle touch to get his attention.

Bladder Control

Imperfect bladder control can also be a part of aging. Long ago I removed all of the wall-to-wall carpeting in my house and replaced it with ceramic tile. If an accident happens it is a simple

Greyhounds love to be stroked.

matter for me to mop it up. Likewise, dog beds should have a plastic-covered foam pad inside with a soft cover outside that can be removed for easy washing. Don't fear that your house will look stark or barren. A few washable or dry-cleanable area rugs can do a lot to soften the overall effect.

ARTHRITIS

Dogs, like people, are prone to arthritis as they age. This is especially true of ex-racers if they had broken bones that perhaps were set imperfectly or not at all. The good news is that nonsteroidal anti-inflammatory drugs (NSAIDS) that are safe for long-term use with Greyhounds are available.

Not that long ago, the only answer to arthritis pain for dogs was either aspirin, which can upset the stomach, or cortisone, which can cause an array of side effects when used long term. This new class of drug can put the zip back into your dog's step and increase his interest in walking and even running. Ask your veterinarian if it would be appropriate for your dog.

ELEVATE THE FOOD BOWL

As a dog ages his trachea becomes less flexible. This can lead to choking and gagging problems, especially if he has to strain to reach down to floor level for his food. Elevating his dish will help enormously.

CHECK BLOOD VALUES

Many medical conditions, such as decreased kidney or liver function, can be detected by having your veterinarian perform a complete blood scan. This should be done yearly on any dog over the age of seven. If a problem is detected early, you may be able to head off trouble with medication or even a change in diet.

SAYING GOOD-BYE

I won't deny that the end of a dog's life is a wrenching experience for an owner. As the head of an adoption agency, I not only have to deal with the passing of my own dogs but also hear of the

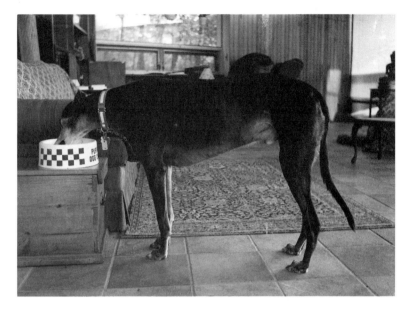

Older dogs especially appreciate elevated food bowls.

passing of dogs that I have adopted out. While it is all very sad, it also has been very meaningful to me. I am constantly moved by how much people love their Greyhounds. It is a wonderful thing.

Whether you have had your dog for two years or twelve, the final good-bye is just as hard. I do not believe that people should ever be told that their dog would be better off euthanized. The decision to euthanize is a very personal one. Most people who suggest euthanasia are just trying to be helpful and to remind you that there is a way to end your dog's suffering—but the final choice is yours alone.

When my dear King was diagnosed with cancer at the age of thirteen-and-a-half, one of my concerns was, How will I know when it is time to let him go? My veterinarian told me, "Don't worry, you'll know." I couldn't imagine how that would be true. And yet, two months later, one day I looked at King, he looked back, and I knew. It didn't make it any less sad, but at least I had the strong feeling that his life at that point involved more pain than pleasure and that he was ready to go. I was with King as the vet administered the final needle, and as he went into the next

The old guard, Jasper (foreground) and King.

world, I told him how much I loved him. That is all we can do for our dogs, but it is no small thing.

Old age for a dog does not have to mean misery either for you or for him. When you reflect on all the pleasure dogs bring you during the course of their life, I'm sure you'll agree that they are worth making a few modifications so that they can maintain their dignity and you can continue to be enriched by their company.

Chapter Six

Insecticides and Anesthesia

*A*s you've probably already realized, Greyhounds are very sensitive creatures. What you may not know, however, is that this sensitivity also extends to their reactions to certain drugs and chemicals. The information in this chapter will help you provide safe relief for your dog from such pests as fleas, as well as enable you to discuss with your veterinarian the anesthesia best suited for Greyhounds should the need arise.

FLEA COLLARS

In our attempt to rid our pets from fleas, we Americans have exposed ourselves, and our animals, to an assortment of toxic chemicals. Take, for example, seemingly innocuous flea collars. They are sold everywhere, and one could almost be lulled into thinking that they are both safe and effective. In fact, they are neither. Standard flea collars have their origins in nerve-gas chemical warfare, and they work by permeating the skin of your animal's neck and, eventually, paralyzing and killing the flea that bites the skin. They should never encircle the neck of a Greyhound nor, in my opinion, any other animal.

Some of the chemicals commonly found in flea collars can, in a Greyhound and other sensitive and/or allergic animals, cause nausea, convulsions and even death.

An added hazard is that we dispose of over *50 million* of these collars every year, which means that they add to the already growing toxic-waste problem we face in this country.

In general, I believe we, as a culture, have become far too casual in our use of toxic chemicals. One look at the state of our air and water will confirm that. So, too, have we become too casual about the chemicals we put on our pets. As it turns out, because of the way their bodies metabolize these substances, Greyhounds are extremely sensitive to many pesticides, so there is no margin for error.

Similarly, the chemical compounds found in various flea shampoos, dips and sprays can be equally deadly.

INSECTICIDES

Most insecticides can be grouped into one of three families: the organophosphates, the carbamates and the pyrethrins. Neither the first nor the second should ever be considered for use on Greyhounds.

ORGANOPHOSPHATES

Some examples of organophosphates are malathion, diazinon and chlorpyrifos (sold as Dursban®), all of which are used in various potent flea killers. As with flea collars, I don't believe any animal (or human) should be exposed to them, but especially not Greyhounds. A recent study conducted at the University of Washington showed that even a single episode of poisoning worthy of treatment could lead to "a persistent decline in neuropsychological performance."

CARBAMATES

The next group, carbamates, includes carbaryl (sold as Sevin®) as well as other carbamate compounds. These, too, hold the potential for a bad reaction, either in the short term with immediate symptoms (such as profuse salivating, labored breathing, vomiting and so on) or in the long term (nervous system damage or cancer).

Pyrethrins

Pyrethrins are the least toxic of the three and are a natural substance derived from the chrysanthemum flower. Pyrethroids (such as permethrin, allethrin and resmethrin) are man-made equivalents. They are strong enough to kill most fleas but have a very low toxicity level for mammals. It is very popular to mix pyrethrins with piperonyl butoxide. This is a synergist that, although toxic, can be used sparingly (combined with pyrethrins) if an infestation is especially severe.

Also to be avoided are chemicals (cythiolate, propoxur and fenthion) that are applied monthly to the length of the dog's spine or in a spot on the base of the neck (sold as Rabon®, Baygon®, ProSpot®, Ex-Spot® and others). They are much too strong for a Greyhound, and you are risking damage or, possibly, death. In general, if a product says "safe for puppies and kittens" it will be safe for a Greyhound.

NEW PRODUCTS

In the last few years several new products to combat fleas and ticks have appeared on the market. The following are safe for Greyhounds, and I would go so far as to say that now there is no need for a dog to ever suffer from these pests again.

Lufenuron

Lufenuron (marketed under the name Program®) is a once-a-month flea reproduction inhibitor. It is not an insecticide and will not kill fleas. However, the eggs produced by fleas that have fed on a treated dog will not hatch. Eventually, if all the pets in a home are treated, home infestation can be prevented. The drawbacks are that it takes a while to work, you must treat all of the animals in a household and the fleas must bite a treated animal for the flea to become sterile. If an animal has a flea allergy (flea dermatitis) it will aggravate the condition. Program should be used in combination with insecticides to improve its effectiveness. The cost of treatment is about $6.50 a month.

Imidacloprid

Imidacloprid (marketed under the name Advantage®), is a topical insecticide that kills fleas on contact, before they can lay eggs, so it breaks the flea life cycle. A few drops are applied once a month directly on the dog's (or cat's) skin. It spreads on the skin's surface and remains effective even after bathing or swimming. The advantage (no pun intended) is that it actually kills the fleas, it works within twenty-four hours and the animal does not have to by bitten by fleas for it to work. The disadvantages are that it is only available from veterinarians and it is rather expensive, about $10.00 a month. Compared to constant flea dipping, exterminators, and relentless house cleaning, though, it seems well worth the price.

Fipronil

Fipronil (marketed under the name Frontline®) is a topical insecticide that kills both fleas and ticks. One application kills fleas on dogs for up to three months and ticks for up to a month. Like Advantage it works within twenty-four to forty-eight hours and is not significantly affected by shampooing or swimming. Its chief advantages are that it kills both fleas and ticks and the cost is reasonable, about $11.00, for an ampule that will kill fleas for three months and ticks for one.

Amitraz

Amitraz is the active ingredient in tick collars marketed under the names of Preventic® and Tick Arrest®. This collar is not to be confused with standard, toxic flea collars. Amitraz is carried in the oils of the dog's skin, paralyzes the mouth of the tick and detaches 99 percent of ticks within twenty-four hours. The collar is good for about seventy-five days, but it is a good idea to remove it before shampooing or letting your dog swim, as these may reduce its effectiveness.

Although the collar is nontoxic to Greyhounds if worn, it is very toxic if they somehow chew on a collar. Make sure the collar is tight enough that it makes contact with the skin. Clip off any excess material once the collar is fastened. If you have more than one dog and they play bite each other's neck, this is not the product for you. The cost of a collar ranges from $10.00 to $18.00, depending on whether you buy from a veterinarian or a retailer.

Although these new products have been tested as safe for Greyhounds, it is possible that your dog may have an allergic reaction. This is true of all drugs and even food. It does not mean that the products are not safe for Greyhounds in general. It just means that you may have an allergic dog.

NATURAL FLEA CONTROL

I know how maddening an infestation of fleas can be, and so here are some effective, nontoxic ways to deal with the problem.

First of all, it is important to treat your home and not just the dog. Fleas come from the environment, so you must eliminate them there. Vacuum daily and throw away the vacuum bag. Wash the dog's bedding frequently. Heat also kills fleas, so you can toss the dog's pillows in a hot dryer.

INSECT GROWTH REGULATOR

A relatively new product, which is called an insect growth regulator (IGR), eliminates fleas by preventing them from reproducing. Given that two adult fleas can produce over one million offspring in a year, it is essential that their reproductive cycle be broken. Generally, the products, which go by the trade names of Precor® and Torus®, are sprayed all over the house and in the animal's sleeping areas. One warning: Sometimes companies combine IGR's with toxic chemicals. Make sure what you buy (or what you have applied by an exterminator) is in its pure form.

One of the 2,237 species of fleas.

HERBAL PREPARATIONS

The only completely safe products to apply directly to your Greyhound's skin are herbal formulas, which vary in effectiveness, and pyrethrins. Most herbs simply drive fleas away but don't kill them. Pyrethrins work by literally choking fleas to death. Pyrethrin formulas are found in powders and shampoos, but read the label carefully and avoid toxic additives.

DIETARY ADDITIVES

Some people use dietary means to control fleas. One woman I know dusts her dogs with brewer's yeast weekly and adds it to the animals' food. Many people report success with garlic capsules. Still others swear by the addition of vitamins. I have tried all of the above with little success. They do serve, however, to bolster your dog's immune system, so, if for no other reason, they may be worth a try.

THE FLEA COMB

There is one sure-fire, totally nontoxic way to keep fleas (and ticks) from your Greyhound. It's by using a flea comb, and while it is anything but a high-tech device, it really works! I comb my dogs (and cats) daily and find that although it is a bit time-consuming, it is a way to groom your animal safely and spend some time with him.

The best way to use a flea comb is to first get set up with two bowls of water: one soapy and warm, the other clear and warm. Then place your pet right next to the soapy water bowl. Now comb through once (with the hair, not against it), and you'll see fleas (if there are any) and flea dirt trapped between the fine teeth of the comb. Immediately dip the comb in the soapy water. The dirt will fall off, and the fleas will drown as the soap clogs their lungs. Make sure the comb is flea free, then rinse in clear water before you make the next pass through the animal's fur. You'll see that the dog will come to enjoy the combing both for the relief it brings and for the time you're spending with him.

HOW TO REMOVE A TICK

Ticks are hard to remove because their mouth parts are barbed and they also secrete a sticky substance that holds the mouth in place while feeding. If you remove a tick incorrectly you will cause it to release the very toxins you are trying to avoid.

Do not use your fingers. Use tweezers or a specially-made tick-removal device. Grasp the tick's body and pull away from the point of attachment. Do not jerk or twist. If the mouth breaks off, use a sterilized needle to remove it as you would a splinter.

Wash the bite area with soap and water, and apply an antiseptic, such as alcohol. Wash your hands thoroughly with soap and very warm water. Mark the date of the tick bite on the calendar and watch for symptoms of disease in upcoming weeks.

DEWORMERS

Ridding your Greyhound of internal parasites (worms) is another area in which you must be careful. Droncit® is the drug of choice for tapeworm (a byproduct of having fleas). Use Droncit in tablet form, rather than administering injections. Not only are tablets cheaper, but they minimize the possibility of a painful injection. Panacur (also called Safeguard®) is best for hookworm, roundworm and whipworm. Task® is definitely not recommended for use against worms in Greyhounds, as it has an organophosphate base. As you now know, Greyhounds are extremely sensitive to this substance, and you could very well create more problems than you would solve. Be sure to make your veterinarian aware of this if he is not already.

Some people routinely deworm their dogs, which constitutes a severe misuse of a toxic substance. Even some veterinarians have been known to dispense dewormers without having performed a fecal test. Dogs should only be dewormed if a fecal sample has been microscopically examined by a veterinarian and found to contain parasites. Dewormers are toxic and can build up in a dog's system over time and irritate his intestines. Furthermore, overuse of dewormers will bring about resistant strains of parasites, much the way antibiotics are overused and have given way to resistant strains of bacteria. The old adage "Kill the worm, not the dog" should be kept in mind. If your yard has parasites which continually reinfect your dog, treat your yard, and keep the dog out of it until the problem is resolved.

ANESTHESIA AND THE GREYHOUND

How they respond to anesthesia is another way in which Greyhounds (and other sighthounds) are different from other breeds of dogs. If you think your veterinarian may not be familiar with these differences, you might want to lend him or her this book so he can read the next section for up-to-date information on the subject.

One reason Greyhounds react as they do to drugs is that their liver metabolizes them more slowly. Another factor is the breed's low percentage of body fat proportionate to its size. Greyhounds have, on the average, 16 percent body weight of fat as compared with 35 percent in mixed-breed dogs of similar weight. The level of some drugs in a dog's system falls by going into its fat. The less fat, the longer it takes for the blood level to fall.

Certain forms of anesthesia are safer than others for Greyhounds. Bear in mind that all anesthesia, whether for dogs or humans, carries some risk. Never avoid necessary surgery because of this risk, but do select a veterinarian who will talk with you and choose the safest type of anesthesia and administer it in the safest way. (Also, when practical, combine procedures such as spaying or neutering with a teeth cleaning. That way a dog only has to be anesthetized once.)

Dr. Alan Klide, associate professor of veterinary anesthesia at the University of Pennsylvania School of Veterinary Medicine, has this to say about anesthesia for Greyhounds: "It is common practice to give a drug to calm dogs before anesthesia is begun and also to give them one to make them dry and prevent the heart from slowing. If Greyhounds are given a higher dose of

A fifteenth-century French print showing Greyhounds being treated by "veterinarians."

narcotic, then they will need less thiobarbiturate. There are many narcotics, but the one that is most useful and safe, in dogs, is called oxymorphone. Glycopyrrolate, one of two drugs used to dry secretions, allows the dogs to wake up sooner than if the other drug, atropine, is used."

THIOBARBITURATES

Further, Dr. Klide suggests:

"This whole problem can be avoided by not using a thiobarbiturate. There are other drugs that can be injected to begin anesthesia. One called methohexital is commonly used by veterinarians to anesthetize Greyhounds. There are two relatively new intravenous anesthetics which look promising for anesthetizing Greyhounds, and these are propofol and ctomidate.

There are several inhaled anesthetics which are used in veterinary and human anesthesia. In general, halothane is well tolerated in normal individuals. A newer anesthetic which may be useful in some circumstances is isoflurane."

My own experience with sighthounds and anesthesia is that recovery seems quickest when isoflurane is used. But not all delays in recovery can be traced to the type of anesthesia used. In some cases when it takes a dog an excessive amount of time to regain consciousness, there is often an underlying problem that delays recovery. Complete blood tests, especially on dogs over the age of five, are a must because many health problems can be detected in advance.

MALIGNANT HYPERTHERMIA

Greyhounds can experience a further reaction to anesthesia. Dr. Klide explains:

"There is a disease of humans and some animals which is rare, but very severe. It has been reported in Greyhounds. It is called malignant hyperthermia. When the individual with this condition is stressed or anesthetized with certain anesthetics, including all the available inhaled ones, they get very hot, may get stiff and will probably die unless they are given a drug called dantrolene. If a dog or its relatives has such a condition in its history, it should be given dantrolene before, during and for a few days after it is anesthetized.

When other drugs such as sedatives or tranquilizers need to be given to Greyhounds, if possible, a low dose should be tried first."

WAYS TO SPEED RECOVERY

To discourage a prolonged recovery in a Greyhound, Dr. Klide notes the following:

- "Intravenous fluids may have to be limited because of heart disease.

- Keep the dog warm; cold prolongs the depth and duration of anesthesia.

- Provide mechanical ventilation if necessary.

- Administer oxygen if necessary.

- Turn the dog periodically to try to prevent the occurrence of pneumonia.

- Measure blood sugar and make normal if not normal."

LAWN CHEMICALS AND CANINE CANCER

One final piece of advice pertains to the use of herbicides on your lawn. There was a time when people (and companies) would use whatever chemicals were needed to rid a lawn of weeds and promote green grass. Not so anymore.

A commonly used weed-killing chemical compound called 2, 4-D has been linked to cancer in dogs. In fact, dogs that walk on treated lawns are twice as likely to develop lymphatic cancer. And, if the lawn is treated four or more times a year, a dog's risk of developing cancer doubles. Studies are now underway to see what health hazards are posed to humans. So, if you value your dog's health (and possibly your own), avoid the use of herbicides on your lawn.

Are your dogs safe from the hazards of herbicides?

If your dog is accidentally exposed to herbicides, wash his paws immediately with soap and water, make sure he doesn't lick his paws and keep an eye on him. If he exhibits any signs of poisoning such as salivating, disorientation or vomiting, take him to a veterinarian immediately.

Chapter Seven

Training

When you adopt a retired racing Greyhound, you are getting a dog that is already extensively trained. The problem is that some of the training is irrelevant to his new life as a companion. As such, there are some new tricks that you must teach this "old" dog as well as some old tricks that you must help him to forget.

It is uncanny how most Greyhounds seem to be right at home even though they've never before been in a house. I've concocted a rather elaborate legend to explain this.

Long ago, in a racing kennel far away, a Greyhound went home for the night with his trainer. He was a very intelligent and very observant Greyhound, because when he went back to the kennel the next day he was able to recount to his fellow racers every detail of what it was like to spend the night in a house. Because he was a Greyhound that was exceptionally fond of pleasure, he gave special attention to details of soft places to sleep and where the food was kept.

Since the other Greyhounds had little to occupy their minds with other than thoughts of chasing the lure, they took great delight in these tales of home life. And so, by oral tradition, the story spread. Mother Greyhounds told the tale to their young pups. Old male Greyhounds told it to young males. Over the years the details of what it was like to live in a house spread to every racing kennel in the land. And that is why Greyhounds behave as if they've waited all their lives for the experience of living with you—because they have!

Ajax carries his pillow everywhere and uses it for—what else?—a head rest!

Unfortunately, over the years some of the story became exaggerated (that Greyhounds are to be fed steak upon request), while other parts were left out entirely (like the fact that not everyone wants a dog on the sofa). So now it is up to you to set the record straight and establish the rules of the house.

HOUSEBREAKING

One rule that everyone will agree on is that the dog must be housebroken. The reason for it is obvious. What is not so obvious to some people is how to accomplish it.

You have a leg up (no pun intended) on the process by virtue of the fact that racing dogs have already been crate trained. In the kennels, Greyhounds are housed in large crates (cages) and are let out four times a day to exercise and relieve themselves. For most dogs it does not take a very big leap of the imagination to see your entire house as a crate.

The first thing you need to do is keep your dog on a schedule. As much as possible, try to adapt yours to his. In other words, if you usually get up at nine in the morning but you know the dog is used to waking at seven, get up earlier at first, then gradually change the dog's sleeping patterns.

TAKE THE DOG OUT OFTEN

The basics of housebreaking apply to racing Greyhounds just like any other breed. Walk the dog first thing in the morning, after both meals, midday if possible, and before bed. Keep an eye on the dog in between, too. If he seems restless and begins pacing, he may need to go out. Bear in mind that the dog may be a little uneasy in his new surroundings, and this, combined with new food and water and a new schedule, may affect his bowels and bladder.

USE THE CRATE

In Chapter Four I talked about the importance of crates in easing the transition from kennel to home. Most of what was said there concerned preventing the dog from hurting himself or becoming destructive in the home. Yet crates are useful tools for housebreaking, too.

Since racing Greyhounds are crate-trained, you can prevent "accidents" in the house by putting the dog in a crate. They have been trained not to soil their crates, and rare indeed is the Greyhound that will.

If you take your dog out four or five times a day, if you keep an eye on him the rest of the time and if the dog sleeps in the crate at night, there is little room for error.

There are exceptions, of course.

I have found that a few modest Greyhounds are uncomfortable relieving themselves while someone is holding them on a leash. You can walk them for miles, but if they know you're there watching, they won't do their "business." Later, this type of dog, in desperation, usually finds a remote corner of the house in which to relieve himself. What should you do? The answer is simple: If you have a fenced yard, let him run loose. But what if you don't? You have three choices: find a fenced area, fence in a small area yourself or require the dog to get used to being on lead. The second or third choices are the ones you will eventually make, because it certainly isn't very convenient to travel to someone else's fenced yard four times a day just so your dog can have some privacy!

If you decide just to tough it out and make your dog comply, then you might consider using an extendible leash so that the dog can get at least 10 or 20 feet away from you. One word of caution, though: Extendible leashes come in a plastic box with a handle. The leash extends from there, much like a tape measure. The design flaw is that it is very easy for it to be pulled out of your hand if the dog gives a sudden lunge. Then not only will your dog be running loose but the noise of the plastic box scraping along the sidewalk may scare your Greyhound into running even more. If you choose to use an extendible leash, make sure you also buy a safety wrist loop that attaches to the plastic handle on one end and over your wrist on the other. The loops are very inexpensive and could save your dog's life.

Extendible leashes are only safe when used with a wrist loop.

BEHAVIORAL "ACCIDENTS"

As to another perplexing housebreaking problem, some "accidents" aren't accidents. The dog is quite intentionally marking his (or her) territory. For this I recommend scolding the dog firmly but gently and putting him in the crate. You must be consistent and react the same way every time. Don't scream. Greyhounds are far too sensitive for that. And, of course, never ever strike him. A serious tone of voice coupled with the crate is all you need to address the problem.

HEALTH PROBLEMS

Don't overlook the possibility that your dog may have developed a health problem. Diarrhea or persistent urinating in the house may be the sign that something is physically wrong. Parasites and urinary tract infections are common causes of housebreaking problems. Before you begin any behavior modifications, eliminate the possibility of a health problem. Have your dog checked by a veterinarian, especially if he was housebroken then suddenly isn't.

If for some reason you choose not to use a crate, keep your dog confined to one room—preferably the kitchen—and spread newspaper on the floor. Bathrooms tend to be too small and can cause a dog to feel claustrophobic and panicky, while basements are generally dark and give the dog the feeling of being shut off from the rest of the house. Many Greyhounds that were wrongly confined to a bathroom or basement have reacted with panic and have tried to gnaw their way out, damaging the woodwork and their mouths in the process. Never put your ex-racer in a garage! Remember, the idea is to acclimate your dog to become a part of the family. Garages are for cars, not for your companions.

OBEDIENCE TRAINING

I recommend a basic obedience course to everyone who adopts an ex-racer. A well-trained dog is a real asset. Not only is he easier to live with, but also he has a very clear idea of his boundaries and becomes comfortable and secure knowing that when he does what you want, you are happy with him. Most dogs, and especially Greyhounds, are eager to please.

A dog's training could also save his life. A dog that is out of control rarely remains with the same family who originally adopted him. Take a visit to any animal shelter and you will see many dogs, purebreds and mixed breeds alike, that never had the benefit of basic training. Sadly, most of them will be euthanized because when people are looking to adopt a dog, the trained ones are the first to be chosen. Should your dog ever have to be readopted, good training is an investment in his future. How many people do you know who would be interested in adopting an older dog that chews shoes, jumps up on people and pulls on the leash?

CHOOSING A GOOD TRAINER

There is no special requirement for a basic obedience course other than that it be accomplished humanely. Greyhounds are extremely sensitive, and if the course instructor believes in shouting, instilling fear, using choke collars with metal prongs or, worst of all, electric shocks, don't walk away, run! I have seen Greyhounds that have endured cruel training, and they have never recovered. Their spirit was broken, and they developed many neurotic habits as a result.

You should also decline to participate in a program if the teachers recommend leaving the dog behind so they can train him alone. A wonderful bond is established between you and your dog when you take an obedience course together. Actually, you are both being trained—you are being trained as the pack leader, and the dog is being trained to look to you for guidance. By leaving the job to someone else, there will always be a missing link. Besides, who knows what kind of training will take place after you've gone home?

The best trainers are the ones who teach a dog by praise rather than fear. Additionally, a trainer should be aware of the temperament differences between breeds and train accordingly. Greyhounds, for example, do not respond to commands the same way German Shepherds do. All lessons should be tailored to the breed.

GETTING THE GREYHOUND TO SIT

Frequently I am asked, "Can Greyhounds sit?" My answer is "Yes, but most of them prefer not to." It isn't painful for them, but I get the distinct impression that it is uncomfortable. Usually you'll find a Greyhound in one of three poses: standing, crouching (with forelegs extended, chest resting on the floor) or lying on his side. There's nothing wrong with any of these postures except that they take up a bit of room. If you insist that the dog be

Bossy proves that Greyhounds can sit!

taught to sit, train him the same way you'd train any other dog. Gently pull up on his collar while pushing down on his rump. He may not get it at first, but with practice he will. By the way, one myth that has been circulating is that racing Greyhounds are trained not to sit so they will leave the starting box quicker. This is not true. Racing dogs are naturally eager to take off, and sitting is the last thing on their minds.

TOOLS OF THE TRADE

THE MUZZLE

All racing dogs are transported with muzzles. In the Introduction, I explained that it is not because Greyhounds are vicious, but, rather, because all dogs are more prone to aggression when they are under stress, be it the stress of chasing a lure or of traveling in close quarters.

When you adopt an ex-racer, the muzzle should be part of his "dowry." It will become an essential part of training him when he first meets your other pets.

Racing muzzles, made of molded plastic, are used only during a race.

When the temperature dips below 32 degrees, Greyhounds need coats.

Most Greyhounds are excellent with small dogs and cats. A few aren't. You don't want to find out which category he falls into the hard way. Exercise caution. Just because the dog is wonderful and affectionate with you, that doesn't mean he wouldn't chase, and kill, a cat. And the fact that he gets along with dogs his own size doesn't mean he would be able to resist catching your toy dog.

Even if you don't have other pets, a muzzle can come in handy in the future. If he is not good about having his nails trimmed, a muzzle is invaluable. Additionally, if he will be running with other dogs in a fenced area, they all should be muzzled.

THE CORRECT COLLAR

When walking your dog on a leash, always use a choke collar. The reason for this is simple: the head of a Greyhound is very narrow, and a regular collar would have to be kept on so tightly that it would choke the dog continually. At the racetrack, leashes are rarely used; the person leading the dog uses the dog's collar as a handle. That way the dog cannot escape. But in life on the outside it is not practical to hold your dog by the collar.

A choke collar will stay slack until the moment it is needed, and only then will it tighten up. You would be amazed at the ease with which a regular collar can slip right over a Greyhound's ears. Before you know it, the dog is gone and you are left holding an empty collar. Some Greyhounds are quite expert at backing out of their collars, too. Regular collars are fine for wear around the house and to hold ID and rabies tags, but some sort of a restraining collar is essential for use on the street. Many people I know keep a choker and leash permanently attached and slip them on the dog as they go out and slip them off when they come in. The people who do this keep a regular collar (with ID tags) on at all times, just in case the dog ever dashes out the door. The choker is used only for walks. There is always the possibility, albeit remote, that a choke collar could get caught on something and actually choke the dog when you aren't around, so it's best to reserve its use for the leash only.

"Humane" Choke Collars

Of the various choke collars on the market, the one I recommend, and indeed the one I give out with each adoption, has a slightly different construction from the traditional choker. It consists of two flat nylon circles, a smaller one intertwined with the larger. When the choke action is needed, it restrains the dog firmly and securely yet never pinches the throat or gags the dog. This type of collar is known generically as either a martingale collar or as a humane choker. As far as I'm concerned, no Greyhound should be without one.

If you choose to use a standard choke collar, make it a flat or rounded nylon one rather than a chain choker. Greyhound skin is too sensitive for the metal ones.

Holding the Leash Properly

While we are on the subject of collars, let me say a few words about leashes. Many people do not hold a leash correctly. There

The collar no Greyhound should be without. Tracey models the humane choker.

Do Wacka Do, 1989 Iowa Distance Champion, shows off a slip-lead for quick release in lure coursing.

is a reason that there is a loop at one end of the leash, and that is so you can put your hand through it. Only once the loop is over your hand and is resting around the outside of your wrist do you take hold of the leash. Holding the leash correctly prevents it from ever slipping out of your hand.

We have come to call the correct way of holding the leash the "Greyhound Grip," and everyone who adopts from us, whether or not they have ever before owned a dog, gets a 10-second demonstration on the right way to hold the leash. Those of us involved in adopting out these dogs are acutely aware of how important it is to hold tight.

As for what type of leash to get, I recommend either four- or six-foot lengths. If your dog is a chewer, try a metal chain leash. Otherwise, nylon or leather will do nicely. There is no particular advantage to the extendible/retractable leash, but the disadvantages are that the dog can get farther away from you and can easily get tangled up around you or something else and the leash, in general, provides less control. And, as I said earlier, they should never be used without the safety wrist loop accessory.

Using a Harness

If you choose to use a harness rather than a collar and leash, fine. A harness does provide good control, but it is somewhat of a nuisance to put on and take off. It should, of course, be taken off when not needed, as it can chafe and irritate a dog's skin. Don't forget to keep the appropriate ID tags, licenses and so on attached to a collar. You never want your dog to be without identification, even at home.

Just because you choose to use a harness doesn't mean you can tie the dog in the yard either on a runner or to a stake. With a dog capable of reaching high speeds in a short period of time, even the snapping back of a harness when the dog reaches the end of his tether could injure him severely.

Most Greyhounds do not pull while on-lead. For the few that do, the best method of control is a no-pull halter. It gives the dog a humane tug under the arms when he pulls too hard and reminds him to stay in line.

Remember, walk a Greyhound on a leash or release him in a completely fenced area only.

This is a chapter that you may want to read over a few times. The information in it comes from personal experiences I have had with these wonderful dogs. If you can learn from some of the mistakes that others have made, then perhaps those mistakes were not in vain. And, once you and your dog have reached an understanding with each other about the way things are, you will have the best companion in the world.

MEETING OTHER DOGS

To introduce your new Greyhound to his new housemates that are dogs his own size (or any size down to about 20 pounds), let them first sniff each other with a closed door between them. Dogs can tell a lot about each other from their scent. Let them have plenty of time to get the full doggy bouquet, then, with both the Greyhound and your other dog on leashes, let them meet. The best place for their first meeting is on neutral territory and, preferably, outside. A lot more sniffing will occur. If you see either dog's hackles rise, move them apart. It is only one Greyhound in a million that will start a fight with another dog, so if either is the instigator, it will probably be your other dog. Gradually they will establish which one is dominant, and they will probably become best friends.

MEETING VERY SMALL DOGS AND CATS

If you have small dogs or cats, bring your Greyhound into the house on a leash and *wearing his muzzle*. This is essential because, as you know by now, Greyhounds are terribly fast. Should they pull the leash away from you, at least you'll have the insurance of a muzzle. I once heard of a couple who adopted out Greyhounds advising new owners not to use the muzzle on the theory that they would be giving the dog a mixed message. They incorrectly thought that by using the muzzle you would be indicating to the dog that it was time to race. Nothing could be further from the truth. The racing muzzles are of a completely different construction from the type you will get, which are used only when the dogs travel or are turned out together. Believe me, the racers know the difference!

I remember that when I adopted my original Greyhound, King, I told the person from whom I took him that if he went after my cats I would have to return him. As it turned out, he was terrified of the cats and trembled and cried during the first month he was with them. Needless to say, we had no trouble. My second Greyhound, Ajax, was totally unafraid and barely acknowledged the cats' existence. No trouble there, either.

Signs of trouble are when the dog actively lunges at the small pets, barks or growls or is just too interested. A certain degree of interest is normal. They are sighthounds, after all, and they respond to visual stimuli. But "too much interest" is when they literally can't take their eyes off the pet, they begin to crouch down as if to spring forward or they whine in the direction of where they last saw the pet. Should you see any of these signs,

Boof Man is so good with small animals he even protects stray kittens.

124

keep the muzzle on and keep the dog on a leash, and under no circumstances should you leave them alone together.

To correct a dog that may see these small pets as prey, use a choke collar, and whenever he attempts to lunge, jerk the collar and firmly say "No." Eventually you will "deprogram" any but the most intractable dog from his racing training. If a dog does not respond to your corrections within a few days, think about exchanging him for a dog that does not have the chasing urge so deeply ingrained. For some dogs, no amount of correcting will work, and you don't want a tragedy on your hands. By the way, even though most dogs eventually will respect the small pets in the house, outside may be a different story. The house, after all, is your domain, but as far as they are concerned, outside is up for grabs. You'll have to teach them otherwise, the same way you taught them inside.

Don't be alarmed by the information you've just read in this section. Most Greyhounds are just fine with small pets. And even the ones that aren't initially can usually be trained into complying. I say "usually," because I believe there are a very few for which the racing instinct is just too strong. There are extreme ways to get a dog to stop chasing, but I prefer taking the dog back and placing it in another home where there will be no temptation. I care for cats and small dogs too much to jeopardize their lives, and I respect the Greyhounds too much to put them through strenuous and unkind training.

RETRIEVING A LOST GREYHOUND

You may recall that in the first chapter I discussed the hazards of intentionally letting an ex-racer run off-lead. There is always the chance, though, that it will happen unintentionally. Of course we can't control everything, but it is prudent to be as careful as possible.

If you experience the misfortune of having a Greyhound run away from you or your yard, there is one way of getting him back that is sometimes more effective than simply calling him. It involves using a device intended for hunting that simulates the sound of an animal in distress. It is usually referred to as a squawker. A similar device is also used at the track when, at the finish line, one of the dogs starts heading in the wrong direction. The sound of the squawker gets his attention there, and it may do the same in your neighborhood. Squawkers are available at hunting supply stores as well as through mail-order catalogs.

There are other steps to take to find your Greyhound besides the squawker. Keep in mind that time is of the essence and many trails go cold after a few days.

The first thing to do is notify the police, the local animal shelter, the animal control officer and any nearby veterinarians (including your own). Stress to them that the dog is a retired racer capable of great speeds and that he is gentle and frightened. Give them your work and home phone numbers, plus the dog's ear tattoos, a physical description of him and any identification he is wearing (adoption group tag number, rabies tag number, dog license number and so on) Make sure you also notify the group from whom you adopted since they may well be the first to get a call from someone who has found him. They may also have volunteers in your area that will be willing to help search or distribute flyers.

Posting and distributing flyers is essential. If you can deliver them door to door, so much the better. Put them in supermarkets, store fronts, vet's offices, anywhere where people congregate.

Children are a great resource because they visit friends in neighborhoods and travel on school buses. They are also frequently in people's backyards, areas where you may not be able to see while searching. Use them as lookouts, and give them your numbers. You might also try contacting local schools to see if they'd be willing to make an announcement over their loudspeakers.

If you have an answering machine, mention your lost dog in your outgoing message and ask people to hold the dog if they've found him. Offering a reward is optional. My experience has been that there are many people in the world who sympathize with losing a dog. They will help you, money or not. The word reward on a flyer may, however, attract attention. Be prepared to pay up if you make an offer.

Since dogs at the track run in ovals, they often travel the same way when they are loose. If you are lucky enough to see which direction he was headed in as he left, track him in ovals or circles. While you are searching for him, it is often helpful to bring other Greyhounds, as the sight and scent of them may lure him to you.

Don't forget to place ads on the radio as well as in newspapers. Phrases like "owner heartsick" or "dog is frightened" strike a chord in other dog lovers and may improve your chances of eliciting help.

Finally, don't give up. We've had dogs on the loose for months that were eventually retrieved (although they caused us many sleepless nights). From time to time replace old signs and flyers with new ones that state that you're still looking. Make sure you list the date of disappearance, location, a complete description of the dog and several numbers where you can be reached. Again, ask people to hold the dog if they find him and stress that he is gentle but shy.

"Invisible" Fencing

Frequently I am asked about fencing that is operated by a radio signal. If a dog crosses a predetermined boundary, a slight shock is delivered to his neck through a special collar. To put it simply, I don't like the system, and here's why.

I feel that racing Greyhounds have had quite enough negative reinforcement training to last them a lifetime. A shock to the neck, no matter how slight, would certainly be too much of a shock to the system for some of the more sensitive Greyhounds that I've met. Besides, I had a salesman of this type of system come to my property once, and I asked to feel the intensity of the shock collar. I put it against my leg (which I believe is less sensitive than a Greyhound's neck) and found it to be quite irritating. While not exactly painful, it was definitely startling and uncomfortable. I sent the man packing.

Another reason is that while these fences supposedly keep dogs in (and even that is up for debate—I once knew a Whippet named Wicket that would run through, shock or not)—they don't keep other dogs, animals or people out. So, a vicious neighborhood dog could come into your "protected" yard and attack your Greyhound. A rabid raccoon could do likewise. And, perhaps worst of all, a person could walk in and steal your Greyhound.

Housebreaking also can become a problem with invisible fencing. Dogs that were once perfectly trained can become so loathe to go outside because of the shock that they wind up doing their business in the house. I have known this to happen when several people did not follow my advice and installed these fences anyway. The dogs eventually were returned to us although we had a bit of a job rehabilitating them.

Finally, the speed with which Greyhounds run means that the length of time they are exposed to the correcting shock of the collar is very short—so short that it may not make a difference to them. Like little Wicket, they'll run through anyway.

HOME ALONE, YES—
IN THE YARD ALONE, NO

Never leave your dog outside in the yard while you are not at home. Let me explain why.

A dog that may be perfectly calm in the yard as long as he knows you are in the house may go into a panic if he sees you drive away. Fear is a powerful emotion, and if the dog thinks he is somehow being abandoned, he is going to do everything possible to get to you. Everything may include jumping the fence, digging beneath it or even managing to unlatch the gate. Believe me, it has happened.

Another potential hazard in leaving a dog unattended in a fenced yard is that another animal may get in. A fight, started either by your dog, that is protecting his territory, or by the intruder, may ensue. Who will be there to break it up?

It's not only animals that can get into your yard. People can, too. It could be someone as innocuous as the meter reader, who doesn't latch the gate properly when he leaves, or it could be someone who steals dogs from unattended yards. There are such people who make their living by stealing dogs for resale to research laboratories.

Finally there is the weather to consider. Greyhounds have poor tolerance for both heat and cold. Think of the days when you leave for work and it is bright and sunny, then, out of nowhere, the clouds move in. Before you know it, the temperature has dropped 20 degrees and you wish you'd taken a sweater with you. Now think of the Greyhound with his thin skin and virtually no body fat. With neither fur nor fat for protection, Greyhounds are strictly indoor dogs.

By the way, while a dog door may be a convenience for you while you are home, make sure you bring your dogs in and lock the dog door before you leave. Many of the above cautions apply if you allow your dogs to go in and out while you're gone. To compound matters, other animals may even come into your house in pursuit of one of your hounds.

FENCING BASICS

Since the vast majority of Greyhounds are not jumpers, a fence 4 feet high will suffice, but never any lower. Remember, though, that the fence must be higher if it is erected on a hillside. The downward slope could give the dog an added height advantage. You will also be pleased to know that most are not diggers. In all of my adoptions, I've placed only four that were climbers, so for them, a chain link fence was out. Stockade or some sort of smooth wood was the only type that they could not climb.

SAFE, INEXPENSIVE FENCING

I am often asked what is the best type of fencing for ex-racers. Ideally, it should be smooth wood, 6 feet in height.

If money is a consideration, there is a safe, inexpensive fence you can install yourself with no tools other than a hammer. The fence is made of heavy green wire which comes in 50-foot rolls 4 feet high and is coated with a dark green vinyl. You need to buy metal stake-type fence posts that are 5 feet high and require no digging. You just hammer them into the ground (1 foot underground, 4 feet above) at regular intervals, about every 8 feet. If you place the stakes too far apart, the dogs can bend the wire down if they jump up on it. The wire is simply unrolled, stretched across your yard and attached to the little hooks protruding from the stakes.

Regardless of the type of fencing you have, always make sure the gates are closed. Don't assume that because they were closed yesterday they're still closed today. Likewise, check your fencing from time to time to be sure it's in good condition. I know from experience that things can happen, even to the best fencing. Always check your fencing after a bad storm. Not only might the fencing itself have been damaged, but fallen limbs from trees can pose a real hazard to your dog. He might well run out of your back door at lightning speed.

Finally, all fences should have a sign attached reminding people to latch the gate. Not only will it make them aware but also offers an added bonus: the fact that you keep large dogs may discourage intruders.

Chapter Eight

Having Fun

The ways in which you can have fun with your ex-racer are limited only by your imagination. In fact, there are certain things you can do with Greyhounds that you can't do with any other breed of dog.

ARTIFICIAL LURE COURSING

Take, for example, artificial lure coursing. A plastic bag (or a rag or pelt) is dragged across a field by a motorized cord on a predetermined course. It is virtually unknown outside sighthound circles, and the reason is that the sport depends on the dog's ability to see the artificial lure and to take off after it. As we know, Greyhounds are sighthounds—they hunt by sight rather than by scent as do most other dogs. A Bloodhound would be distinctly nonplussed at the sight of a white plastic bag being dragged across a field. In fact, when he could no longer see the bag, it would lose what little interest it held initially.

Not so with sighthounds. To them, a white plastic bag whipping across a field is enough to make them quiver in anticipation. It stirs up thousands of years of genetics (plus whatever training your racer had at the track) and is a sport made to order. Coursing as a sport grew out of the sighthounds' method of hunting. Not only do they hunt by sight, but they are also used to working as a team with others of their kind. Coursing makes use of both skills.

The Requirements

Specifically, the way a lure-coursing trial works is this:

All events held under the auspices of the American Sighthound Field Association (ASFA) or the American Kennel Club (AKC) allow the eleven sighthound breeds recognized by the AKC to compete: Afghan Hounds, Basenjis, Borzoi, Greyhounds, Ibizan Hounds, Irish Wolfhounds, Pharaoh Hounds, Rhodesian Ridgebacks, Salukis, Scottish Deerhounds and Whippets. The dogs must be at least a year old and registered with the American Kennel Club or the National Greyhound Association.

Since you have a former racer, the latter applies. In most circumstances you will not be able to get a copy of your Greyhound's NGA volume and certificate number. What you must do is apply to the AKC for an Indefinite Listing Privilege (ILP). This is not the same as an AKC breed registration, but it does allow a dog to compete in both ASFA- and AKC-sanctioned lure coursing events as well as AKC obedience trials, tracking tests and herding events. An ILP will only be issued to spayed or neutered dogs. Complete information is available from the AKC (address in Appendix Three).

Coursing events are held on an open field far from traffic and other hazards of civilization. All dogs must be kept on a leash or crated unless they are competing. On the day of the event, each hound that has been entered to participate must be present for roll call. At that time, all the hounds are checked for lameness and, in the case of bitches, to see if they are in heat. If either condition is present, the hound is excused, and the entry fee is returned. Dogs that have dew claws, and almost all racers do, must have them taped to their legs so that they do not become tangled in the cord that pulls the lure.

Next, a random drawing takes place to determine the order in which the breeds compete. Only dogs of the same breed compete with each other (in other words, Greyhounds with Greyhounds, Borzois with Borzois and so on) and are run in groups of three (trios). If necessary, two dogs run together. After the preliminary course, during which each dog will have run twice and earned a certain number of points, another random draw is conducted to determine the order of breeds for the final courses. Dogs that have run together the first time around are not necessarily paired during the finals.

THE JUDGING

After the finals, the dogs with the highest scores compete with each other, and the winner of that course is designated Best of Breed. All dogs are ultimately working toward the title of Lure Courser of Merit, but that requires many points and many competitions. The main thing is to have fun and to watch your dog enjoy himself.

Lure coursing is an especially exciting sport because the dogs are judged by more than one criterion. A dog can get up to 100 points from each course, and the breakdown of maximum points per category is as follows:

Enthusiasm	15 points
Follow	15 points
Speed	25 points
Agility	25 points
Endurance	20 points

As you can see, this sport is not just about speed. Some of the dogs exhibit tremendous concentration (follow) and are distracted by nothing. Others excel in agility. This is seen when the lure is on a straight path and then abruptly takes a turn. An exceptionally agile dog can take a turn without missing a beat.

THE ACTION

At the start of the course, the hounds that have been selected to run together are each given a blanket of a different color. Their collars are removed, and a quick-release collar (known as a slip-lead) is substituted. The trio is lined up at the starting line, and

Getting ready to slip the hounds.

the owner or handler straddles the dog's back. The Huntmaster confirms that the dogs and the Lure Operator are ready. When the Huntmaster says the "T" sound of "Tally Ho!" the dogs are released (slipped).

The Lure Operator has an important job because it is up to him to make sure that the lure is just far enough ahead of the dogs so that they don't actually catch it, yet not so far that they lose interest. The Lure Operator must also be ready at a moment's notice to stop the lure should a dog accidentally get caught in the cord.

Most lure courses are between 500 and 1400 yards long. The cord is set out on an irregular course and is run through pulley stakes that are driven into the ground. There are several ways in which a dog can get injured during coursing, although all are relatively rare.

It is possible for a dog to get his foot caught in the cord. That could result in anything from a rope burn to a pulled tendon to a broken bone. Another hazard is that it is possible for dogs to collide. An extreme outcome of that could be a serious injury, but most likely a bumped dog will simply be thrown off course and lose time (and points).

CAUTIONS ABOUT COURSING

After getting you enthused about lure coursing, let me add some words of warning. Lure coursing is an extremely strenuous sport, and I believe the vast majority of ex-racers should not be involved with it or, if they are, not for too long. There are many reasons for this.

First of all, your Greyhound was retired for a reason. If he is five years of age or older, he was probably beginning to slow down after having had a winning career. Greyhounds are retired around that age because strenuous exercise is too hard on them at that point. This does not mean their lives are almost over, it just means that they are more suited to less taxing pursuits like long walks in the park.

If your Greyhound is younger than five, why was he retired? It is not always possible for the adoption agency to find out the exact cause of retirement; often they are just told the dog was not fast enough. But why wasn't he fast enough? Did he have an underlying medical condition that slowed him down or perhaps an undetected injury? Some injuries, such as a broken leg or dislocated toe, are obvious, but others do not show up until the dog is really active. By then it may be too late. If you are not absolutely certain why your Greyhound was retired, then a complete physical examination by your veterinarian, including blood tests and possibly X rays, is in order.

Not all coursing fields are equal, either. Many sighthound breeds have a better innate ability to maneuver sharp corners than do Greyhounds. To compound it, our ex-racers were trained almost from birth to race in an oval pattern with no turns at all. Some courses are laid out with extremely sharp turns, which could seriously injure your dog if he doesn't do it right. Additionally, since most coursing fields are not fenced, they need to be well away from heavily traveled roads. Not all are. Don't believe it when people say that your Greyhound will be so transfixed by the lure that he'll never run away. I've seen it happen more than once.

I am sorry to say that I know of many people who have not exercised caution and who have coursed ex-racers with disastrous results. Some have coursed dogs that were overweight, some have coursed dogs that were too old and some have coursed dogs too often in a day. Some of the blame for this falls on a coursing club that will allow such practices. Unfortunately, inexperienced clubs and enthusiastic owners are a bad combination, and some dogs that were supposed to be enjoying their retirement years have been gravely injured.

Some clubs use the excuse that they are coursing just for fun, not for competition. What they fail to understand is that the dogs are completely unaware of whether or not their owner will get a ribbon or a trophy at the end of the session. All they know is that the lure is in motion and they're going after it. Greyhounds run even if it is not in their best interest. They will overcome pain to run, and they will ignore poor field conditions (hard ground, rutted or slippery surfaces and so on) or inclement weather (too hot, too cold or too humid). They depend on you, their guardian, to know right from wrong. I know that the sight of your hound chasing across a field is awe inspiring, but put your dog's welfare ahead of your entertainment. You owe him that much.

I have heard it said that a dog can injure himself even in his own backyard. This is true. But injuries are more likely on the coursing field. Also, no matter how fast your Greyhound tears around the backyard, it will neither be as fast nor with as much determination as when he is in pursuit of the lure.

To sum up, coursing is a wonderful sport best left to younger dogs, dogs that are exercised regularly (not just every other Sunday), and dogs that have been certified in good condition. The coursing club you participate with should be well experienced both in the operation of the lure and in first aid. Also, a veterinarian should be on call in case of a serious injury. People in charge of experienced clubs did not learn by trial and error. They learned from other experienced people and were smart enough to take their advice. The coursing field should have

The chase.

Catching up with the "lure," three white plastic bags.

gentle, manageable turns for Greyhounds, and it should be far from traffic.

AMATEUR RACING

Amateur oval racing is another sport that is limited to sighthounds and it may be less taxing on former racers. These events, regulated by the National Oval Track Racing Association (NOTRA), run the dogs on an oval or u-val (U-shaped) track. Greyhounds and Whippets are considered the major breeds, while the other sighthounds are considered minor breeds.

Whippets and the minor breeds use the u-val track, while Greyhounds and Whippets use the oval track. The track surfaces are dirt or grass, and great care is taken to make sure they are very level. Continuous loop equipment pulls an artificial lure around the track, and dogs are judged on the order of the finish.

As a dog wins more heats (races) he accumulates more points, which lead to the Oval Racing Championship title (ORC). Points depend not only on where your dog finishes in a day's standing but also on how many other dogs competed that day as well as how many other dogs already have earned an ORC title.

Greyhounds and Whippets must use a starting box for oval racing. They must also be muzzled during the race and know how to use a starting box (no problem for an ex-racer). Because dogs can reach higher speeds on a track than on a lure course, even greater care must be taken to make sure that your dog is fit.

FUN RUNS

Another alternative to lure coursing adopted ex-racers is fun runs, sometimes organized by the adoption groups and other times just an informal gathering of enthusiastic owners. By getting ex-racers together in a large, fenced area such as a ball field, your dog can exercise and commune with others of his own breed while you can socialize with people with whom you have a lot in common—your love of these dogs.

To ensure the safety of your dog, I recommend strongly that the following safety tips be observed:

1. Have a vet examine your dog to make sure he is in good health and free of hidden injuries.

2. All dogs must be muzzled. If you have ever seen a dog fight you would understand this. Once aggression starts there is no stopping it, and all dogs, even the most mild mannered, will join in the fray.

3. Only ex-racers should be allowed to run—and not more than two dogs at a time. Even dogs that are "friends" while on-lead with their owner can become competitive while running free in a fenced area.

4. Make sure there are no small dogs or cats in the area. Even dogs that live with small creatures in the house may go after them outside. They don't need teeth to hurt them either. A sharp blow from a paw might be enough to break a small animal's back.

5. Do not allow your dog to run during the hottest time of the day or in very humid weather. Have fresh water available at all times, and make sure you walk the dog after he runs to help him cool down. Bring along a first-aid kit, too.

6. Always clean up after your dog.

A GREAT JOGGING COMPANION

Another activity that is a natural for Greyhounds is jogging—not alone, of course, but with you. While Greyhounds basically are sprinters, as opposed to long-distance runners, they can build up the necessary endurance if it is done gradually. In fact, the one thing you'll have to watch for is that the dog does not try to run too fast and burn himself out. It's a whole different thing for them to learn to lope along. Also, the pads on the dog's feet may be tender, so start out on soft surfaces, such as grass.

Whole books have been written on the subject of running with your dog, and you would do well to read at least one of them before you get started. Important health tips are included, as well as information on how to build up your dog's stamina.

Purina has, in recent years, sponsored the Purina Hi Pro K-9 Fun Run. The specifics of the runs vary from city to city, but they generally feature a 1-mile walk/run and, for the more physically fit, a 2-mile run. If you and your Greyhound jog together regularly, you both would probably enjoy running with other people and dogs. And imagine your dog's surprise when he realizes that other dogs run, too!

RUN FOR CHARITY OR FUN

Many Greyhound adoption groups hold an annual run for adopters and their dogs. Some do it for the fun of it, while others do it to raise money for the rescue program. If the group you adopted your dog from doesn't have one, why don't you suggest it (and be the one to organize it)?

SHOWING YOUR GREYHOUND

Showing your Greyhound in American Kennel Club–sponsored shows is not an option for two reasons.

First, spayed or neutered dogs do not qualify, and your dog almost certainly has been altered. Remember, the purpose of showing is to breed the "best" dogs afterward, and breeding is not the idea behind adopting an ex-racing Greyhound.

Second, it is difficult, and in most cases, impossible, to get the registration papers for your dog. A dog without papers is also ineligible for showing.

There is an alternative, however. My group, Make Peace With Animals, has an annual event called the Greyhound Homecoming, a picnic attended by all of the Greyhounds, accompanied by their new families, that were adopted through us. One popular event during the day is the Dogs of Distinction ceremony. "Judges" award certificates for such categories as Longest Tail, Biggest Ears, Whitest Teeth, Oldest and so on. The idea, of course, is that all the dogs have something unique to offer and that each one is a winner. And that, too, is the idea behind adopting. Other adoption groups hold similar gatherings, and yours can too.

OBEDIENCE TRIALS

Don't be upset about your dog's truncated show career—cheer up! He can still compete in obedience classes. For that you must get an AKC Indefinite Listing Privilege number and proof that the dog has been spayed or neutered.

If you decide to pursue obedience, get a good trainer who is kind and who understands retired racers. Greyhounds are a quick study, and generally do quite well in obedience.

VISIT THE ELDERLY OR INFIRM

You can have fun with your ex-racer and do a good deed at the same time by taking him to visit hospitals and nursing homes. Many institutions recognize the therapeutic value of such visits.

Elderly shut-ins enjoy a visit from Alexandra, a Greyhound, and Paco, a Chihuahua.

141

My own adoption group, Make Peace With Animals, has a program called AmbassaDogs®, and we have discovered that,
because of their docile nature, Greyhounds are ideal visitors.
Two requirements, of course, are that the dogs be housebroken
and obedience trained. Some facilities also require that dogs pass
the AKC-administered Canine Good Citizen program. It is a very
moving experience to sit quietly with an older person or someone who is ill, watch them pet a Greyhound and see the joy on
their face. Again, if your adoption group doesn't have such a program, why not initiate one?

THE GREYHOUND HALL OF FAME

In Abilene, Kansas (also the home of the National Greyhound
Association), there is a museum dedicated to the Greyhound.
Any dyed-in-the-wool Greyhound enthusiast must consider this
the equivalent of Mecca. While the emphasis is on racing, there
are interesting educational exhibits about the history of the
breed, as well as examples of art depicting the Greyhound. A side

The Greyhound Hall of Fame in Abilene, Kansas.
(Photo: Greyhound Hall of Fame)

treat is meeting Derby, a retired racer that has found a second career as the official mascot of the museum.

ADOPTING MORE GREYHOUNDS

If you're like most people who adopt a Greyhound, you'll soon find that one is not enough. I'm sure your adoption group will be happy to accommodate you. Before you proceed, keep in mind the original traits you were looking for (cat-safe, good with kids and so on) as well as how many dogs you can reasonably afford in terms of time and money. Also remember that two dogs can become competitive over food, toys and attention. Feed them separately, take away toys when you're not around to supervise and make sure you give your existing Greyhound an extra amount of affection once the new dog arrives. One way you might find the right second dog for you is by asking your adoption group if you can foster a dog for them. By having a trial run, you'll know for sure if the new Greyhound will fit into your existing household.

SPREAD THE WORD ABOUT ADOPTION

Finally, here is another way to have fun and get more people interested in adopting Greyhounds. You will discover very soon after adopting that people will constantly stop you and your dog on the street and say one of two things: "What kind of dog is that? He's so beautiful!" or "Is that one of those racing Greyhounds I've heard about?"

What you can do is this: always be prepared with either a descriptive brochure about adopting or with cards giving the name and number of someone who can be contacted for adoption information. You'll be amazed at the number of people who have always wanted an ex-racing Greyhound but didn't know where to get one. Although it is a lot of fun to sing your dog's praises, Greyhounds, being the wonderful dogs that they are, make even better spokesdogs than you could ever be. And remember, for every card or brochure you hand out, there is the possibility that you will have helped a dog in dire need find the loving home he deserves.

Appendix One

Other Sighthounds

Afghan Hound

Basenji

Borzoi

Ibizan Hound

Irish Wolfhound

Italian Greyhound

Pharaoh Hound

Rhodesian Ridgeback

Saluki

Scottish Deerhound

Whippet

Appendix Two

The Greyhound's Anatomy

1 Nose.	9 Loin.	17 Pastern, or
2 Muzzle.	10 Rump.	metacarpus.
3 Stop.	11 Hock.	18 Wrist, or carpus.
4 Apex of skull.	12 Pastern.	19 Elbow.
5 Neck.	13 Toes.	20 Shoulder.
6 Withers.	14 Stifle, or knee.	21 Cheek.
7 Back.	15 Chest.	22 Flew.
8 Hip.	16 Forearm.	

Appendix Three

Adoption Groups, Organizations and Resource Directory

Note: The following is a list of all known Greyhound adoption groups worldwide. **Inclusion does not signify endorsement.** (List courtesy of the Greyhound Project.)

ADOPTION GROUPS

UNITED STATES

ALABAMA

Greyhound Pets of America/Central Alabama
P.O. Box 11184
Montgomery, AL 36111
334-409-0622

Greyhound Pets of America/Northern Alabama
1000 John Rogers Drive
Birmingham, AL 35210
205-833-6654

Retired Racers Adoption Center
℅ Mobile Greyhound Park
P.O. Box 43
Theodore, AL 36590
334-653-4900

ARIZONA

Arizona Adopt A Greyhound, Inc.
2325 East Marmora
Phoenix, AZ 85022
602-971-6935

Arizona Greyhound & Animal Rescue
8987 East Tangue Verde
Box 153
Tucson, AZ 85749
602-749-0833

Greyhound Adoption League
4310 South Calico Lane
Tucson, AZ 85746
602-578-2792
602-322-9095

Greyhound Pets of America/Arizona
P.O. Box 1879
Cottonwood, AZ 86326
520-646-5157

Greyhound Pets of America/Phoenix
7146 North 58th Drive
Glendale, AZ 85302
602-915-0174

ARKANSAS

Greyhound Pets of America/NW Arkansas
17042 West U. of A. Beef
   Farm Road
Fayetteville, AR 72604
501-433-9961

Mid-South Greyhound Adoption Option
P.O. Box 2088
West Memphis, AR 72303
501-758-9076

CALIFORNIA

Dogworks
8724 Toyon Court
Gilroy, CA 95020
408-847-8054

Greyhound Club of America
4280 Carpinteria Avenue
Carpinteria, CA 93013
805-684-4914

Greyhound Friends for Life
Box 620863
Woodside, CA 94062
800-446-8637

Greyhound Pets of America/California
P.O. Box 2433
LaMesa, CA 91943
619-443-0940

Greyhound Pets of America/California— Orange County and Greater Los Angeles
9642 Bay Meadow Drive
Huntington Beach, CA 92646
714-962-0789

*Greyhound Pets of
America/California—Riverside
and San Bernadino*
5687 Galaxy Lane
Mira Loma, CA 91752
909-685-8302

*Greyhound Pets of
America/Northern California*
P.O. Box 641
Fresno, CA 93709
209-298-2029

Hemopet/Pet Life-line
17672A Cowan, #300
Irvine, CA 92714
714-252-8455

Needle Nose Crew
4905 Basswood Lane
Irvine, CA 92715
714-786-0835

Northcoast Greyhound Support
1571 Horrell Avenue
McKinleyville, CA 95519
707-839-4765

Operation Greyhound
272 Chicory Lane
El Cajon, CA 92021
619-588-6611

*Retired Greyhound Adoption
Service (Regas)*
P.O. Box 99
Palo Cedro, CA 96073
916-474-1618

Retired Racers, Inc.
6027 Valley Sage Road
Acton, CA 93510
805-269-2544
818-347-3407

COLORADO

Colorado Greyhound Adoption
P.O. Box 33455
Northglenn, CO 80233
303-452-6269

*Colorado Greyhound
Companions, Inc.*
P.O. Box 271789
Ft. Collins, CO 80527
970-207-1074

Greyhounds as Pets, Inc.
P.O. Box 6999
Colorado Springs, CO 80934
719-633-0171
800-RITE-PET

Recycled Racers, Inc.
6200 Dahlia Street
Commerce City, CO 80014
303-288-1591

*Rocky Mountain Greyhound
Adoption, Inc.*
9935 Elizabeth Street
Thornton, CO 80229
303-452-8574

CONNECTICUT

Plainfield Pets
137 Lathrop Road
Plainfield, CT 06374
203-564-5640
203-564-3391

REGAP of Connecticut
P.O. Box 76
Bethany, CT 06525
203-393-1673

We Adopt Greyhounds (WAG), Inc.
P.O. Box 519
Cheshire, CT 06410
203-288-7024

FLORIDA

Adopt a Greyhound of Central Florida, Inc.
2000 Seminole Boulevard
Casselberry, FL 32707
407-699-4510

Adopt A Florida Greyhound, Inc.
6500 Southwest 42nd Street
Palm City, FL 34990
561-220-0031

Brandywine Downs Greyhound Adoption
1299 Northwest 73rd Terrace
Ocala, FL 34482
352-873-2727

Ebro Greyhounds as Pets
6558 Dog Track Road
Ebro, FL 32437
904-234-3943, ext. 112
800-345-4810, ext. 112

G.R.E.A.T. (Greyhound Rescue And Options of Tampa Bay)
P.O. Box 16775
Tampa, FL 33687
813-971-4732

Greyhound Adoptions of Florida, Inc.
P.O. Box 390221
Deltona, FL 32739
904-789-8180
407-366-0006

Greyhound Pets of America/Central Florida
991 Fulton Lane N.E.
Palm Bay, FL 32905
407-723-9444
407-242-9010

Greyhound Pets of America/Daytona Beach Kennel Club
2201 International Speedway Boulevard
Daytona Beach, FL 32120
904-239-3647

Greyhound Pets of America/Greater Orlando
P.O. Box 151021
Altamonte Springs, FL 32715
407-332-4754

Greyhound Pets of America/Florida Southeast Coast
3808 Gulfstream Road
Lake Worth, FL 33461
561-965-9581

Greyhound Pets of America/Gainesville
2720 Southeast 39th Place
Gainesville, FL 32641
904-375-0761

Greyhound Pets of America/Largo
12286 Mallory Drive
Largo, FL 34644
813-595-7852

Greyhound Pets of America/Naples, Ft. Meyers
11551 Deal Road
North Fort Myers, FL 33917
813-731-3187

Greyhound Pets of America/Tampa Bay
8851 15th Way North
St. Petersburg, FL 33702
813-577-3387

Greyhound Rescue of Tallahassee, Inc.
P.O. Box 13314
Tallahassee, FL 32317
904-878-1204

Greyhounds as Pets of Northeast Florida
P.O. Box 54249
Jacksonville, FL 32245
904-389-2934

Hollydogs Greyhound Adoption
1600 South Dixie Highway
Hollywood, FL 33020
954-925-7758

Humane Society of North Pinellas, Inc.
3040 State Road 590
Clearwater, FL 34619
813-797-7722

Humane Society of Seminole County
2800 County Home Road
Sanford, FL 32772
407-323-8685

Lake Whippet and Greyhound Rescue
570 Myrtle Street
Sanford, Fl 32773
407-321-5893

*The National Greyhound
Foundation, Inc.*
P.O. Box 929
Homosassa, FL 34487
352-628-2281

Pensacola Greyhound Park
951 Dog Track Road
Pensacola, FL 32506
904-455-8595

Pet Greyhounds, Inc.
25 Sand Dollar Drive
Ormond Beach, FL 32176
904-441-2317

Ponce Animal Clinic
18295 Southwest 160 Avenue
Miami, FL 33187
305-254-0715

REGAP, Inc.
P.O. Box 41307
St. Petersburg, FL 33743
813-343-4824

Sarasota Racing Dog Rescue
P.O. Box 18153
Sarasota, FL 34276
941-379-3278

Saving Grace Rescue
1314 Thomasville Road
Tallahassee, FL 32303
904-222-3117

Second Chance for Greyhounds
10826 Dean Street
Bonita Springs, FL 33923
941-947-2365

Valentine Rescue
1134 Harrison Avenue
Panama City, FL 32401
904-763-1627
904-747-1020

GEORGIA

Atlanta Greyhound Adoption
1491 Berkeley Lane
Atlanta, GA 30329
404-634-4883

Companion Greyhounds, Inc.
122 Davis Lane
Marrietta, GA 30068
770-850-1717

Greyhounds Galore
Route 20
Box 404A
Macon, GA 31211
912-742-0474

*National Sighthound Rescue &
Adoption, Inc.*
2399 Fredonia Road
Thomasville, GA 31792
912-226-7632

IDAHO

Greyhound Pets, Inc.
1900 Millview
Coeur d'Alene, ID 83814
208-765-3115
800-228-7794

*Greyhound Pets, Inc. (Boise
Affiliate)*
10273 MaCaw Court
Boise, ID 83704
208-377-0645

*Greyhound Pets of
America/Inland Empire*
5100 Allamar
Boise, ID 93804
901-635-2053

ILLINOIS

Central Illinois REGAP, Inc.
P.O. Box 3625
Peoria, IL 61612
309-745-5377

Chicago REGAP
7751 West Addison
Chicago, IL 60634
312-625-5545

Greyhound Pet Connection
P.O. Box 458
Woodstock, IL 60098
815-568-8403

Greyhound Racers Recycled
1660 Kingsdale Road
Hoffman Estates, IL 60195
847-882-2188

Illinois REGAP
P.O. Box 7044
Villa Park, IL 60181
708-495-0074

*Kountry Greyhound Rescue
And Adoption*
20236 Capp Road
Morrison, IL 61270
815-772-2888

*Midwest Greyhound Adoption,
Inc.*
P.O. Box 338
Sugar Grove, IL 60554
708-466-4022
708-851-3402

Peoria Greyhound Rescue
729 East Bel Aire Court
Peoria, IL 61603
309-685-6818

Racers Recycled, Inc.
4207 Broadway
Quincy, IL 62301
217-223-0187

INDIANA

Central Indiana REGAP, Inc.
7945 East 100 North
Greenfield, IN 46140
317-462-0019

Greyhound Companions of Indiana, Inc.
51115 County Road 7 North
Elkhart, IN 46514
219-264-9708

Greyhound Guardians
3224 Rustic Lane
Crown Point, IN 46307
219-736-1959

Greyhound Rescue and Adoption
8677 South State Road 243
Cloverdale, IN 46120
317-653-5690
317-745-1710

Life After Racing Greyhound Adoption
7201 East 100 South
Whitestown, IN 46075
317-769-5634

USA Defenders of Greyhounds, Inc. (USA DOG)
P.O. Box 1256
Carmel, IN 46032
317-244-0113

IOWA

Bluffs Run Adoption Program
Box 396
Pacific Junction, IA 51561
712-622-8341
712-622-8334

Dubuque Greyhound Park Adoption Program
P.O. Box 3190
Dubuque, IA 52004
319-582-3647

Greyhound Pets of America/Midwest
2397 Utah Avenue
Thor, IA 50591
515-378-3183

Quad City REGAP
301 Cypress Street
Blue Grass, IA 52726
319-381-2676

REGAP
All Pets Animal Clinic
3257 West Fourth Street
Waterloo, IA 50701
319-234-7511

KANSAS

Pups Without Partners
9700 Leavenworth Road
Kansas City, KS 66112
913-299-9797

TLC Greyhound Adoption
323 2400 Avenue
Solomon, KS 67480
913-655-2208

WGP Adoption Center
1500 East 77th North
P.O. Box 277
Valley Center, KS 67147
316-755-4000

KENTUCKY

*Greyhound Pets of America/
Southern Ohio Valley*
P.O. Box 19666
Louisville, KY 40259
502-339-7004

*Greyhound Rescue And
Adoption/Kentucky Chapter*
P.O. Box 99913
Louisville, KY 40269
502-493-0457

Homes for Hounds, Inc.
688 Walker Park Road
Richmond, KY 40475
606-623-6045

*Mid-South Greyhound Rescue
Adoption Option*
4702 Wolf Creek Parkway
Louisville, KY 40241
502-895-8765
502-228-4756

LOUISIANA

*Greyhound Pets of
America/Louisiana*
106 Pineoak Drive
Covington, LA 70433
504-893-0966

MAINE

*Greyhound Placement Service
of Maine (Kennel)*
Box 682
Mount Henry Road
Bridgton, ME 04009
207-647-8944

MARYLAND

The Ark for Greyhounds
11011 Old Frederick Road
Thurmont, MD 21788
301-898-7519

*Greyhound Pets of
America/Maryland*
P.O. Box 42103
Baltimore, MD 21284
410-252-7555

Greyhound Rescue
6397 Woodburn Avenue
Elkridge, MD 21227
410-796-2803

*Midlantic Greyhound
Adoption League, Inc.*
Box 136
Clarksville, MD 21029
301-854-0816

MASSACHUSETTS
Adopt a Greyhound, Inc.
682 Sandwich Road
Falmouth, MA 02541
508-540-0635

*Greyhound Adoption of
Western Massachusetts*
97 Blueberry Hill
Longmeadow, MA 01106
413-567-9022

Greyhound Adoption Service
16 Jak-Len Drive
Salisbury, MA 01952
508-462-7973

Greyhound Friends, Inc.
167 Saddle Hill Road
Hopkinton, MA 01748
508-435-5969

Greyhound Friends West, Inc.
5 Baldwin Hill Road
Great Barrington, MA 01230
413-528-5548

Greyhound Options, Inc.
12 Barnes Street
Ware, MA 01082
413-967-9088

*Greyhound Pets of
America/Massachusetts*
P.O. Box 1495
Middleboro, MA 02346
617-472-4055

Northeast Animal Shelter
204 Highland Avenue
Salem, MA 01970
508-745-9888

*Wonderland Greyhound Park
Adoption Program*
190 VFW Parkway
Revere, MA 02151
617-284-1300

MICHIGAN
Greyhaven
797 West Pickard Road
Mount Pleasant, MI 48858
517-772-5097

*Hav-A-Heart Greyhound
Rescue and Adoption*
877 East McGregor Road
St. Louis, MI 48883
517-681-2028

*Michigan Greyhound
Connection*
P.O. Box 2340
Dearborn, MI 48123-2340
800-398-4364

Michigan REGAP
P.O. Box 1611
Belleville, MI 48112
800-GO-HOUND (for
Michigan only)

NGAP Michigan Affiliates
P.O. Box 19195
Kalamazoo, MI 49019
616-344-9090

also
8517 La Point Drive
Brighton, MI 48116
810-468-2881

*Second Chance for Greyhounds
of Michigan*
P.O. Box 2438
Portage, MI 49081
616-349-5104

MINNESOTA

*Greyhound Pets of
America/Minnesota*
P.O. Box 49183
Minneapolis, MN 55449
612-785-4000

Rochester REGAP
1235 West Center Street
Rochester, MN 55902
507-287-0478

Twin City REGAP
P.O. Box 131963
St. Paul, MN 55113
612-487-1076

MISSOURI

Greyhound Companions
102 Turf Court
St. Louis, MO 63119
314-962-9899

The Greyhound Foundation
43 History Court
Wentzville, MO 63385
314-398-5227

Greyhound Pets of America
P.O. Box 3693
Springfield, MO 65804
417-883-8156

Kansas City REGAP
7400 East 102nd Street
Kansas City, MO 64134
816-763-3333

Rescued Racers
10929 St. Henry Lane
St. Louis, MO 63074
314-423-4126
314-921-7379

St. Louis REGAP
P.O. Box 25383
St. Louis, MO 63125
314-894-0834

MONTANA

Greyhound Pets of America/Rocky Mountain
P.O. Box 447
Billings, MT 59103
406-245-8262

NEVADA

Greyhound Pets of America/California—Nevada
6607 Shelter Lane
Las Vegas, NV 89103
702-251-1934

NEW HAMPSHIRE

Fast Friends
P.O. Box 674
West Swanzey, NH 03469
603-357-7376

Greyhound Pets of America/Central New Hampshire
P.O. Box 6006
Manchester, NH 03108
603-798-5042

Greyhound Pets of America/New Hampshire
P.O. Box 6024
Keene, NH 03431
603-363-4426

Greyhound Placement Service Of NH, Inc. (Kennel)
P.O. Box 58
Mount Vernon Road
New Boston, NH 03070
603-497-2148

REGAP of Seabrook, Inc.
P.O. Box 1861
Seabrook, NH 03874
603-474-3065, ext. 207

NEW JERSEY

Greyhound Friends, Inc.
170 Township Line Road
Belle Mead, NJ 08502
908-874-0508

Greyhound Rescue, Inc.
P.O. Box 365
Fanwood, NJ 07023
908-754-8342

Make Peace with Animals— New Jersey
100 Princeton Road
Parlin, NJ 08859
732-727-5698
732-721-5023 (Fax)

NJGAP
335 County Road 513
Califon, NJ 07830
908-832-9678

NEW MEXICO

Greyhound Companions Of New Mexico
P.O. Box 22053
Albuquerque, NM 87154
505-281-7295

A Place for Us Greyhound Rescue
194-A County Line Road
Englewood, NM 87015
505-281-9799

NEW YORK

Buffalo Greyhound Adoption
149 Keller Avenue
Kenmore, NY 14217
716-873-1165

Greyhound Pets of America/New Hampshire
35 Nelson Street
Fairport, NY 14450
716-377-6815

Greyhound Adoption of Central New York
302 Third Street
Liverpool, NY 13088
315-457-7989

Greyhound Rescue Society
P.O. Box 472
Sugar Loaf, NY 10981
914-651-3580

Greyhounds as Companions
23 Lake Avenue
Nassau, NY 12123
518-766-9173
518-768-2579

Homestretch Greyhound Adoptions, Inc.
317 Perry Street
Schenectady, NY 12306
518-372-7024
518-584-3780

Long Island Greyhound Transfer, Inc (L.I.G.H.T.)
89 Pengon Circle
East Meadow, NY 11554
516-735-6037
516-735-6073

Make Peace with Animals—New York
529 Centre Island Road
Oyster Bay, Long Island NY
   11771
516-922-1852
516-922-2095 (Fax)

NORTH CAROLINA

Circle of Friends Greyhound Adoption and Sighthound Rescue
1058 North Main Street
Walnut Cove, NC 27052
910-591-8867

Greyhound Friends of N.C.
422 Bradford Drive
New Bern, NC 28569
919-637-1731

Greyhound Friends of North Carolina
P.O. Box 514
2908 Oak Ridge Road
Oak Ridge, NC 27310
910-643-0233

Greyhounds Going Home
336 Windsor Manor Way
Kernersville, NC 27284
910-996-4121

Greyhounds of Distinction
P.O. Box 5692
Wilmington, NC 28403
910-251-1414

Homes for Hounds
5120 Davis Road
Waxhaw, NC 28173
704-843-4052

Racers Reward, Inc.
630 Union Street
Concord, NC 28025
704-788-1935

Sanford Animal Hospital
P.O. Box 2157
Sanford, NC 27330
919-775-7946

Triangle Greyhound Adoption
10220 Durant Road
Raleigh, NC 27614
919-847-5533

OHIO

Greyhound Adoption of Ohio
7122 County Lane
Cleveland, OH 44023
216-731-3096

Greyhound Pets of America/Wheeling Downs
P.O. Box 391
Martins Ferry, OH 43935
304-232-4492
304-232-5050, ext. 217

Greyhound Placement
8379 Martingale Lane
Russell, OH 44072
216-338-1744

Lake Erie Greyhound Rescue
278 North Broadway
Geneva, OH 44041
216-466-1347

Ohio Friends of Greyhounds
3921 Logan Northwest
Canton, OH 44709
330-492-3859

OKLAHOMA

*Greyhound Pets of
America/Oklahoma*
7275 East 59th Street
Tulsa, OK 74105
918-496-2301
918-224-3376

OREGON

Adopt-a-Greyhound
4801 Jasper Road
Springfield, OR 97478
503-746-GREY

*Greyhound Pets of
America/Northwest*
P.O. Box 6524
Portland, OR 97228
503-253-5699

Greyhounds for Pets, Inc.
1075 St. Charles Way
Sherwood, OR 97140
503-625-7916

Homes for Hounds
5081 Southwest Pacific
   Highway
Waldport, OR 97319
503-563-3464

Multnomah Kennel Club
P.O. Box 9
Fairview, OR 97204
503-667-7700, ext. 133

Oregon Greyhound Rescue
2207 Northeast 79th Avenue
Portland, OR 97213
503-257-7220
503-236-5071

PENNSYLVANIA

Going Home Greyhounds
181 Spruce Haven Drive
Wexford, PA 15090
412-935-6298
412-781-5946

Greyhound Club of America
540 Sunset Drive
MR #2
Baden, PA 15005
412-935-3276

*Grey-Save of Northwestern
Pennsylvania*
P.O. Box 8612
Erie, PA 16505
814-796-4504
814-825-7825

Make Peace with Animals
P.O. Box 488
New Hope, PA 18938
215-862-0605
215-862-2733 (Fax)

*Monica's Heart Greyhound
Adoption*
1408 East Hamilton Lane
Altoona, PA 16602
814-942-1906
814-943-3145

NGAP
8301 Torresdale Avenue
Philadelphia, PA 19136
215-331-7918

*NGAP of Northwest
Pennsylvania*
P.O. Box 10002
Erie, PA 16514
814-456-4969

Nittany Greyhounds
1146 Ardrey Hollow Road
Port Matilda, PA 16870
814-692-7614

Personalized Greyhounds
128 Old Ford Drive
Camp Hill, PA 17011
717-761-3317

RHODE ISLAND

*Lincoln Greyhound Adoption
Program*
1600 Louisquisset Park
Lincoln, RI 02865
401-781-6231

SOUTH CAROLINA

Carolina Greyhound
213 Meetze Avenue
Lexington, SC 29072
803-957-3866
803-279-6198

*Low Country Greyhound
Adoptions*
14 Harbor River Road
Horse Island, SC 29920
803-838-2550

The Sanctuary
619 Pinecrest Drive
Seneca, SC 29678
864-985-1791

TENNESSEE

*Greyhound Pets of
America/Central Florida*
6511 Sevierville Park
Knoxville, TN 37920
615-573-0837

*Greyhound Pets of
America/Midsouth*
R.R. 1, Box 1
Ripley, TN 38063
901-635-2053

*Tennessee Alliance for
Greyhounds, Inc. (Tag, Inc.)*
P.O. Box 362
Loudon, TN 37774
423-458-6710

TEXAS

Corpus Christi Greyhound Track Adoption Program
P.O. Box 9087
Corpus Christi, TX 78469
512-289-9333

Greyhound Friends for Life, Texas Affiliate
Route 1, Box 233-A8
Canyon, TX 79015
806-499-3511

Greyhound Pets of America/Austin
P.O. Box 200724
Austin, TX 28720
512-258-2947

Greyhound Pets of America/Central Texas
P.O. Box 40086
Georgetown, TX 78628
512-930-9195

Greyhound Pets of America/Houston
P.O. Box 741176
Houston, TX 77275
713-866-4466
713-667-3802

Greyhound Pets of America/North Texas
3037 Dothan
Dallas, TX 75229
214-243-3285

Greyhound Pets of America/Texas—San Antonio
P.O. Box 750
Helotes, TX 78023
210-695-8441

Greyhound Rescue of Austin
7611 Old Bee Cave Road
Austin, TX 78735
512-288-4480

Greyhound Rescue Society of Texas, Inc.
R.R. 1, Box 130C
Hillsboro, TX 76645
817-582-0364

Gulf Greyhound Adoption
P.O. Box 488
LaMarque, TX 77568
800-275-2946
409-986-9500, ext. 2108

Hill Country Greyhound Adoption
430 Flint Rock Lane
Seguin, TX 78155
210-303-2229

Racers Recycled, Inc.
Box 270107
Houston, TX 77277
713-665-3366

UTAH

Greyhound Gang
P.O. Box 274
Kanab, UT 84741
801-644-2903

2nd Chance Greyhounds
11757 South 7th
East Draper, UT 84020
801-571-2439

VERMONT

Greyhound Rescue of Vermont, Inc.
569 Roosevelt Highway
Colchester, VT 05446
802-879-7696

VIRGINIA

Greyhound Pets of America/Virginia
306 Breckenridge Court
Berryville, VA 22611
703-955-0252

Greyhound Pets of America/Virginia–Richmond
P.O. Box 70811
Richmond, VA 23255
804-272-9651

Greyhound Pets of America/Wheeling Downs–Northern Virginia
P.O. Box 8171
Springfield, VA 22151
703-450-6554
703-658-9656

NGAP Virginia Affiliate
636 Piney Point Road
Virginia Beach, VA 23452
804-463-6861

WASHINGTON

Greyhound Friends Northwest, Inc.
1095 Northwest Firwood Boulevard
Issaquah, WA 98027
425-392-9114

Greyhound Pets of America/Emerald Pacific
1812 216th Avenue Court East
Sumner, WA 98390
253-862-4401

Greyhound Pets of America/Inland Empire
4910 North Karen Road
Otis Orchards, WA 99027
509-927-8002

WEST VIRGINIA

Greyhound Pets of
America/Wheeling Downs
1 South Street
Wheeling, WV 26003
304-323-5050

Tri-state Greyhound Adoption
Program & Rescue Center
P.O. Box 7118
Cross Lanes, WV 25356
304-776-1000
304-776-8530

West Virginia Greyhound
Adoptions
P.O. Box 202
Charlton Heights, WV 25040
304-779-9122

WISCONSIN

Fox Valley Greyhound Network
55 Welcome Circle
Appleton, WI 54915
414-731-8838

Geneva Lakes Kennel Club
Adoption Center
P.O. Box 650
Delavan, WI 53115
414-728-8000
800-477-4552

Greyhound Pets of
America/Southeast Wisconsin
7532 Four Mile Road
Franksville, WI 53126
414-681-3200

Greyhounds Only, Inc.
P.O. Box 85
Franksville, WI 53126
414-886-7787
847-731-2511

St. Croix Meadows Adoption
Center
2200 Carmichael Road
P.O. Box 750
Hudson, WI 54016
715-386-4869
612-436-5050

CANADA

NOVA SCOTIA

Greyhound Pets of Atlantic
Canada
7 Lake Front Drive
R.R. #1, Site 8 C-32
Porters Lake, NS B0J 2S0
Canada
902-829-3306

ONTARIO

Adopt a Greyhound of Central Canada, Inc.
R.R. #3
North Gower, ON K0A 2T0
Canada
613-489-0654

Greyhound Club of Canada
R.R. #2
Princeton, ON N0J 1VO
Canada
519-458-8429

Greyhound Lovers of Hamilton Wentworth
3600 Golf Club Road
R.R. #1
Hannon, ON L0B 1P0
Canada
905-692-5790
905-692-4454 (Fax)

Niagara Greyhound Adoption, Inc.
110 South Street North
P.O. Box 283
Port Robinson, ON L0S 1K0
Canada
905-384-1222

Zephyr Farm
R.R. #1
Baltimore, ON K0K 1C0
Canada
905-342-3391

QUEBEC

Greyhound Rescue of Montreal
9240 Charles de la Tour
Montreal, PQ H4N 1M2
Canada
514-389-6186

ENGLAND

Evesham Greyhound Rescue
7 Hinton Road
Childswick, Broadway WR12 7HY
England
011-44-38-685-3971

Finch, Anne
5 Greenways
Egham, Surrey TW20 9PA
England
011-44-78-443-6845

Greyhound Rescue
Derwent View
Brackenholme
Near Selby, North Yorks, YO8 7EL
England

Greyhound Rescue
Newtown Hope
Mansel Ross on Wye,
Herefordshire HR9 5TS
England
011-44-98-975-0643

*NGRC Retired Greyhound
Trust*
24/28 Oval Road
London NW1 7DA
England
011-44-81-335-3016

*Romford Greyhound Owners
Association*
226 Hilldene Avenue
Harold Hill
Romford, Essex RM3 8DB
England
011-44-70-834-5767

WALES

Greyhound Rescue
10 Penmaen Terrace
Mount Pleasant, Swansea SA1
    6HZ
Wales
01792-472-196

IRELAND

Greyhound Friends of Ireland
Glenlohane
Kanturk, County Cork
Ireland
353-29-50014
353-29-51100 (Fax)

GERMANY

Greyhound Rescue Group
Langgasse 22
66989 Hoheinod
Germany
011-496-33-3596

AUSTRALIA

Adopt a Greyhound
91 Prince Charles Road
French's Forrest, NSW 2086
Australia
02-9451-0323
02-9351-3337

Sandown Veterinary Clinic
P.O. Box 13
Springvale, Victoria 3161
Australia
03-9547-6666

ORGANIZATIONS

American Kennel Club
5580 Centerview Drive
Raleigh, NC 27606
919-233-9767
For registration only.

American Kennel Club
51 Madison Avenue
New York, NY 10010
212-696-8200
Headquarters, all other
business.

Greyhound Club of America
4280 Carpenteria Avenue
Carpenteria, CA 93013
805-684-4914
For AKC-registered
Greyhounds.

*National Greyhound
Association*
R.R. 3, Box 111B
Abilene, KS 67410
913-263-4660
Racing organization and
registry.

ADVOCACY GROUPS

The Fund for Animals
200 West 57th Street
New York, NY 10019
212-246-2096

The Greyhound Project
261 Robbins Street
Milton, MA 02186
617-333-6655

Greyhound Protection League
P.O. Box 620863
Woodside, CA 94062
800-446-8637

*NEAVS (New England
Anti-Vivisection Society)*
333 Washington Street
Boston, MA 02135
617-523-0181

*PETA (People for the Ethical
Treatment of Animals)*
P.O. Box 42516
Washington, D.C. 20015
202-337-7382

COURSING/NOTRA RACING ASSOCIATIONS

AKC Lure Coursing
1235 Pine Grove Road
Hanover, PA 17331
717-632-6806

*American Sighthound Field
Association*
1098 New Britain Road
Rocky Hill, CT 06067
860-563-0533
Artificial lure coursing.

*National Oval Track Racing
Assoc. (NOTRA)*
13765 South 1300 West
Riverton, UT 84065
801-254-6817

PUBLICATIONS

Celebrating Greyhounds
P.O. Box 173
Holbrook, MA 02343
617-333-6655
Quarterly magazine for own-
ers, adopters and friends.

The Greyhound Review
R.R. 3, Box 111B
Abilene, KS 67410
913-263-4660
Monthly magazine of the
National Greyhound
Association.

The Sighthound Review
10177 Blue River Hills Road
Manhattan, KS 66503
785-485-2992
Bimonthly magazine about
show Greyhounds and other
sighthound breeds.

ACCESSORIES

Animal Magnetism
P.O. Box 101
Lambertville, NJ 08530
800-836-2546
Mail order, all sighthound
supplies, including specially
made coats for Greyhounds,
humane choker collars, slip
leads for coursing, etc., as well
as books and gifts.

R. C. Steele
1989 Transit Way
Box 910
Brockport, NY 14420
800-872-3773
Mail order, discounted prices
on dog crates.

$\mathcal{I}$ndex

INDEX